REMEMBERING CHAPEL HILL

REMEMBERING CHAPEL HILL

THE TWENTIETH CENTURY AS WE LIVED IT

VALARIE SCHWARTZ

THE History PRESS

Published by The History Press
Charleston, SC 29403
www.historypress.net

Front cover image: Work by Chapel Hill tapestry artist Elaine O'Neil (www.elaineoneil.com).
Back cover image: Map by Mary C. Dirnberger, UNC class of 1929, drawn in 1933.

First published 2009

Manufactured in the United States

ISBN 978.1.59629.704.3

Library of Congress Cataloging-in-Publication Data

Schwartz, Valarie.
Remembering Chapel Hill : the twentieth century as we lived it / Valarie Schwartz.
p. cm.
Includes bibliographical references.
ISBN 978-1-59629-704-3
1. Chapel Hill (N.C.)--History--20th century. 2. Chapel Hill (N.C.)--Biography. I. Title.
F264.C38S39 2009
975.6'565--dc22
2009021530

Contents

Contents

Preface

In my mind I'm goin' to Carolina
Can't you see the sunshine?
Can't you just feel the moonshine?
Ain't it just like a friend of mine
To hit me from behind.
Yes, I'm goin' to Carolina in my mind.

The words of James Taylor's "Carolina in My Mind," above, and the power of the University of North Carolina (UNC) Tar Heels on the basketball court may be the first associations that some people have with Chapel Hill, but the true spirit, as with any town, lives within its people. Transient as any college town, many people stay long enough to acquire the degree they seek and then leave; others come for various reasons and find it difficult to leave. Others still, sometimes natives, leave an indelible mark before moving forward in their lives, as with James Taylor, who spent his childhood and developed his musical talent here; Kay Kyser and Andy Griffith, who were educated here; and the young men who enter the basketball program. *Remembering Chapel Hill* provides a glimpse at the town that grew around the nation's first state-funded university and the ways that some of the people who lived here during the twentieth century affected or were affected by it.

It takes a village to raise more than a child, and even though this book was based on some of the "Neighbors" columns I wrote for the

Chapel Hill News, it would not have been furthered without the village mentality of generosity and caring that remains strong and proud in Chapel Hill. Everyone approached for historic photos or information had something to offer, if only the name of another person to ask. Leads and encouragement were not only invaluable, but also great, humbling reminders that this book, though it carries my name, is only possible through the generosity of those willing to open their homes, hearts and memories in the name of preservation of our history. To everyone mentioned in *Remembering Chapel Hill*, as well as those along my journey, please accept my deep gratitude (in no particular order): Billy Barnes, Jock Lauterer, Lillian Lee, Roland Giduz, Velma Perry, Esther McCauley, Shirley Van Clay, Glenda Hargraves, Peter Rashkis, Ann Simpson, Tracy Chrismon, James Carpenter, Virginia Taylor, Jeanette Fearington, Richard Hart, Charles Holloway, Cat Williams, Ann Sullivan, Keith Longiotti, Betsey Giduz, Elaine O'Neil, Jennifer Pendergast, Thomas Hughes, Ernest Dollar, Traci Davenport, Doug Eyre, Don Evans, Bill Burk, Eleanor Cobb Wiles, Clarence Whitefield, Bitty Holton, Michael Brown, Noreen Ordronneau, Mary Harley Kruter, Bill Burk, Vicky Scott, Joe Nassif, Penny Haith, Susan Riley, Sharon Campbell, Mary Pringle, Beth Hildebrand, Charles Mack, Steve Scroggs, Kip Gerard, Laurie Norman, Chris Kanoy, Sara Gress and Nerys Levy; and to those who nurtured me and persevered during the process: John, Mary, June, Jonathan, Sally, Kirk, Janine, Jane, Michele, Elaine, Nina, Carmela, my book club neighbors and, finally, Cosmo—my constant companion and the only one of many great Chapel Hill dogs to make it into the book.

PART I

THE EARLY YEARS

As I saw Franklin Street in 1912 it was a dusty red avenue cut through a forest of magnificent trees. The road dipped through a valley and then rose, but the trees dominated the scene and obscured any buildings that then existed on that section of Franklin Street. My first impression of Chapel Hill was trees; my last impression is trees.
—Robert Burton House, UNC class of 1916; first chancellor, 1945–57, as he arrived as a student in 1912

Chapel Hill might have forever been lost among the trees and no more than a pretty picnic and hiking spot near a crossroads had it not attracted searchers looking for a place on which to bring forth the University of North Carolina. The United States was in its infancy in 1789 when the North Carolina legislature voted to begin the nation's first state-funded school of higher education. To make it available to all one hundred counties of the formerly Old North State, it needed to be centralized yet far enough away from alluring distractions like, say, Raleigh or Hillsborough, which were the capital and an established county seat, respectively, in central North Carolina at that time. (Durham, which is about twelve miles northeast of Chapel Hill, would not become much more than a small settlement with a train depot until after the Civil War.) Various areas were explored before a chunk of land—mostly on a rocky Orange County hill in a settlement known as New Hope Chapel Hill—was identified as ideal. Amid a forest of longleaf and loblolly pines, holly, dogwood, redbud, oaks, maple, shagbark hickory and other

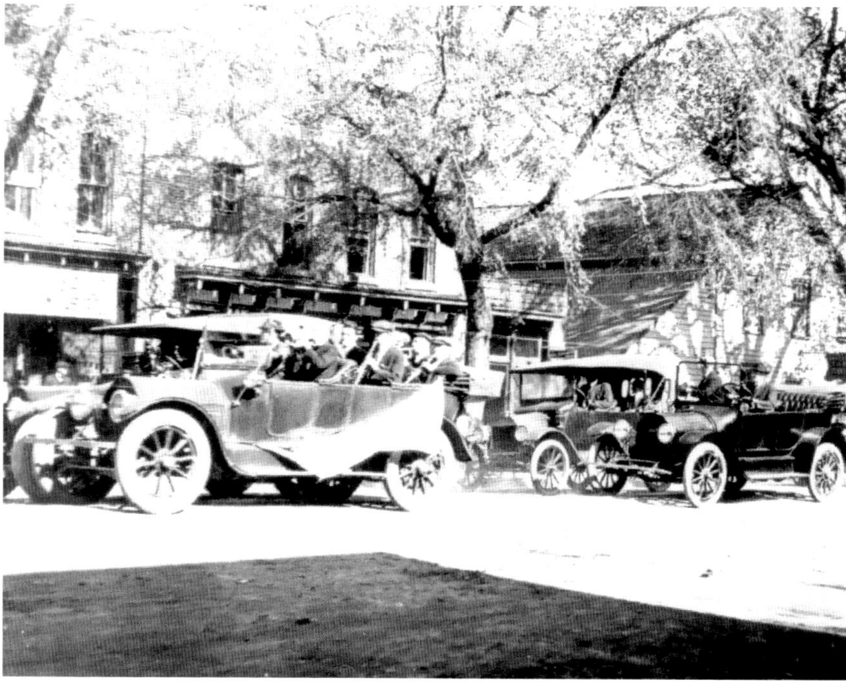

This parade took place about 1910 on East Franklin Street near the intersection with Columbia. Notice the unpaved street and immature trees. *Courtesy North Carolina Collection, University of North Carolina Library at Chapel Hill.*

evergreen and hardwood trees, a simple, abandoned log chapel stood on that hill, near the site of today's Carolina Inn.

During the summer of 1792, a contingent of trustees led by William R. Davie, one of North Carolina's most constructive thinkers at the time, rested on the hill under a robust tulip tree (*Liriodendron tulipifera*), or yellow poplar. Archibald Henderson, a lifelong resident of Chapel Hill and Kenan professor of mathematics, wrote:

> *All alumni of the University are familiar with the story that, on a warm summer day, exhausted by their searches for a suitable site, a group of Trustees headed by Davie sat down to rest upon the luxuriant grassy lawn beneath a giant poplar standing near the crest of the ridge popularly known as Chapel Hill. Beneath the poplar's umbrageous limbs the weary Trustees regaled themselves with exhilarating beverages; and after partaking of a picnic lunch and a refreshing nap,*

> *they unanimously decided that it was useless to proceed further, the eloquent Davie having convinced them that no more beautiful or suitable spot could be found elsewhere.*

Cornelia Phillips Spencer has been credited with naming the giant tree the "Davie Poplar," and through great preservation efforts it remains a campus treasure to this day despite damaging lightning strikes and hurricanes.

Subsequent outings by school founders brought the mapping out of what the campus would look like, and along the northern border, on a flat spot of the hill, was designated the town of Chapel Hill, which, as the campus grew, became the center of commerce and residence for those employed to construct it and later to teach and learn in it. The main street was aptly named after Benjamin Franklin, a founding father of our new nation with abilities that matched his curiosity and led him to great discoveries, much like so many who have traversed Franklin Street through the years. Chapel Hillians would certainly agree that "an investment in knowledge always pays the best interest," among many of Franklin's other famous quotes.

The last decade of the nineteenth century saw the South continuing to dig itself out of the shambles wrought by the Civil War. The university (affectionately called "Carolina") was one of only two Southern colleges that had remained open during the conflict, but racial issues continued for some years through Reconstruction, tearing people apart. By the time of its centennial celebration during commencement in 1889, the campus and town had mostly recovered and have continued to progress.

In 1896, running water was installed on campus, though an old open privy could still be found more than a dozen years later. Townspeople augmented their incomes or, in the case of some widows, supported themselves entirely by turning their homes into boardinghouses. Professors and administrators of the university were traditionally the most financially secure of those living in Chapel Hill, though they carried long notes on the large, now historic homes that they built, many of which have been preserved and restored and continue to add southern charm to the town today. Money has always been tight for most of those associated with the school, bringing fundraising for programs, departments and new ventures into the landscape, along with the faith and courage to continue trailblazing.

Nell Pickard

Miss Nell Pickard was born February 10, 1899, on Pickard Farm at White Cross, eight miles from Chapel Hill. The youngest of nine children—two boys and seven girls—she moved with her family to Chapel Hill in 1904 (one year after telephone service began in town) into the house at 114 South Columbia Street, next door to University Baptist Church. "It wasn't much different living there than the country because Chapel Hill was so small back then," Pickard said. Many years and extensive renovations later, that house is the Beta Theta Pi fraternity house.

Her father, George Pickard, ran a livery stable with hacks and buggies for carrying students back and forth between the university and the train stations in Carrboro and Durham before he later became superintendent of grounds at UNC.

George Pickard was highly respected in the community. An editorial after his death in August 1924 concluded, "It would be hard to convince people in Chapel Hill that God ever made an honester man than George Pickard."

Miss Nell, as everyone called her, laughed after hearing the above line and said, "He was the Democrat of the county. Anything the Democrats wanted passed, they came to him." He served as county commissioner, town alderman, a member of the county board of education and a representative of Orange County in the state legislature.

His will stated that his property was to be divided among his unmarried children. Six daughters qualified.

In 1925, Nell and her sisters commissioned the building of the house on the corner of Rosemary and Boundary Streets. She and her sisters lived in it until their deaths, with Nell as the last survivor. (She died there on June 20, 1997, four months after her ninety-eighth birthday and the interview for this story.) Only one sister married, and the rest went to work or college. Miss Nell was in the first class of women to graduate from

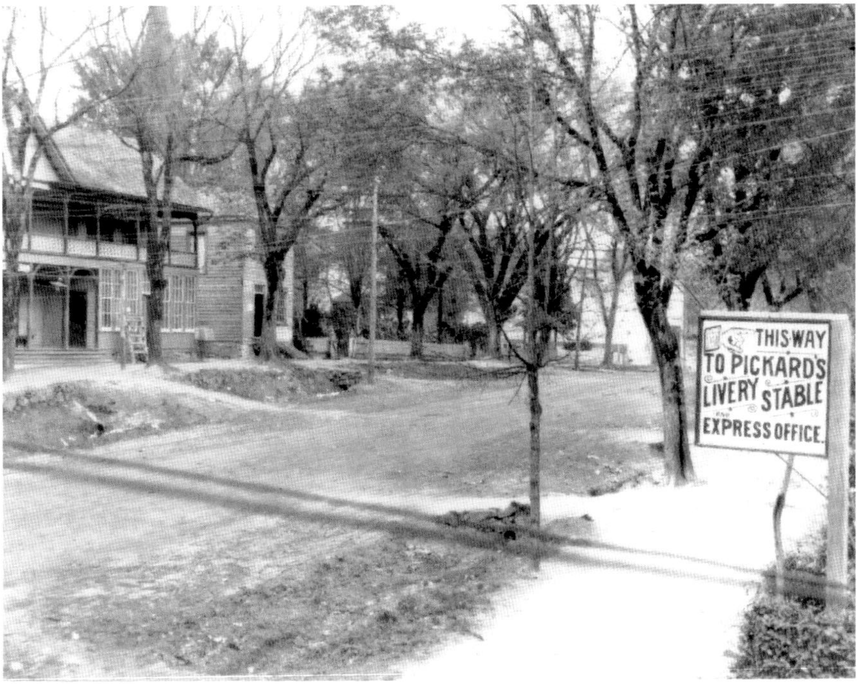

This circa 1900 photo taken looking west on Franklin Street at Henderson Street shows the way to the livery stable owned by Miss Nell Pickard's father. *Courtesy North Carolina Collection, University of North Carolina Library at Chapel Hill.*

UNC who had matriculated as freshmen. "Three of us local girls were admitted, two from Chapel Hill and one from Carrboro, but only two of us graduated in 1921. I majored in Modern Languages." There were other women at the university who had transferred in from other schools, and the first female law students were also admitted at this time.

Nell's nephew, Dallas Pickard of Durham, was at a gathering with his wife, Mary, to celebrate Nell's birthday, and he shared stories about his aunt while munching on homemade cake and cookies. "She was on the first UNC women's basketball team," he said.

"That's right," she concurred, "but I played on the second string. We wore bloomers and navy midi tops with high-laced tennis shoes." After graduation, she taught French in public schools around the state for ten years. But she really missed Chapel Hill. "There's no place like Chapel Hill," she said.

"I used to read a lot and traveled a good bit. I went to Europe three times, went to Canada and Mexico, and I would go to the Kentucky Derby." A friend chimed in with, "And when we couldn't go to the Derby we'd just have mint juleps."

"My aunt has been blessed with two good things," said Dallas Pickard, "a strong constitution and very caring ladies who take care of her." Then he named the seven women who arranged their schedules so someone was with her at all times. Lois Burnette had been with her for twelve years and cooked her meals. "She'll eat anything I cook." But one of Nell's favorites was Brunswick stew. Dorothy Bynum, Elizabeth Russia, Ida Paris (who made the birthday cake) and Rhonda Atwater took turns coming in, and Carolyn Evans slept there every night. Lucy Marsh, who was with her nine hours a day, four days a week, said, "I've worked with elderly people for thirty years. Miss Nell is the oldest and she's a miracle. I'm just so proud of her."

During the Depression, in the early 1930s, Miss Nell stopped teaching and went to work at the university until her retirement in 1964. She was the secretary to Dean Carlton Spruill of the General College and at one time worked in the undergraduate admissions office.

"I remember when I used to sit in my office on the third floor of Old South and turn my chair and look into the window of East Building. I could remember before East was born and could never have believed there would one day be a building with an antenna there."

She wore a beautiful turquoise dress that stunningly set off her white hair. Libby Daniel, who came to know Miss Nell through her years of work at the Horace Williams house down the street, said, "You see, don't you, that she doesn't have a line on her face." She was right. Okay, maybe a few, but less than any of the rest of us. Waiting around long enough, secrets emerge, and soon she spoke of the only explanation she could give for a face without wrinkles—Elizabeth Arden moisturizer. "Whenever I've used anything on my face, it was Elizabeth Arden."

Clemmie Flowe Thompson

Like most who have lived in Chapel Hill, Clemmie Flowe Thompson was not born here. She moved to Chapel Hill from her family home in

Charlotte with her husband, Bill, at the age of twenty-eight. She and Bill boarded at Mr. Strowd's house.

"Mr. Strowd was the postmaster and he had a three-story house on Davie Circle—well, it wasn't Davie Circle then; he owned the 1,200 acres surrounding it," said Thompson. The year was 1924, and they lived in the most eastern portion of developed Chapel Hill, considered out of town at the time. The East Franklin Street hill that must be traversed when entering the town from the northeast (the direction of Durham) is called Strowd's Hill.

At the time of this interview, Thompson was the oldest resident at Carol Woods Retirement Community. She celebrated her 100th birthday on December 10, 1996. Her husband, who spent forty-four years in the banking business, worked for the Bank of Chapel Hill, which later became North Carolina National Bank and then, just before he died in 1971, NationsBank. "Bill worked at the branch in Carrboro until Roosevelt closed all the branch offices. It was quite a commute to Carrboro." They owned a Ford coupe for the long drive (of about two miles) from their house on Vance Street.

The Thompsons joined University Presbyterian Church in March 1926. Thompson actively participated in the Women's Circle No. 1 and served on the properties and flower committees. "I don't go to church any more because there aren't many cars that my wheelchair will fit into," she said. She was among the first to move to Carol Woods when it opened in 1979. After Bill's retirement in 1963, they lived in the Estes Drive house that they custom built and she landscaped, where her hydrangeas still grow. "The woman who lives there now brought me some flowers from it last year. They are such a beautiful blue!"

She had prepared for company; her hair looked lovely, and she had powdered her face and rouged her lips. Tastefully dressed in a silk, gray print dress, an interesting multistranded silver necklace accented it. Childhood memories have become her favorites as the last remaining of seven children. She remembers the three-room schoolhouse that the Baptists built where "even grown men would come to school" because it was a private school. She remembers the day that she went to school at age six (1902) and someone was giving the children shots.

"I didn't want to be vaccinated for smallpox! I was scared and started crying so they didn't vaccinate me. They told my father he could come over and get the needles and vaccinate all of us. So he did," she recalled. She grew up on a farm "out from Charlotte" that provided all their needs except for coffee and sugar. "We were raised to work and do what we could and enjoy doing it. Even now, I do everything for myself that I can possibly do," which is more than her doctor would like. "He doesn't want me to do a thing." It is a point of great pride for Miss Clemmie that she can take care of herself, doing everything except putting weight on her feet.

"I haven't been sick a day in my life. I never drank alcohol or smoked cigarettes. I was brought here to the third floor for diagnosis. I was having bad dreams and had a lot of falls, but I didn't break anything until I broke my hip. I've got a pin in one, but they can't put a pin in the other because my bones are crumbling."

This is a woman who truly understands independence. She and Bill raised two sons. Bill Jr., born in 1924, "died too young, when he was sixty-seven," she said with resignation. Her other son, called Dickie, was two years younger than Bill Jr. and was born with a severe birth defect.

"He had no muscle use," said her great nephew, Avery Phillips of Charlotte, in a phone conversation. "He couldn't do anything. Sometimes you could tell he was smiling; he was somehow able to communicate things to them. They both took care of him. Uncle Bill would stay with him so she could go to her meetings."

She was a longtime member of the Chapel Hill Woman's Club, is a charter member and past treasurer of the Chapel Hill Garden Club, is a member of the Chapel Hill Historical Society and was a volunteer worker for a number of years with the Chapel Hill Inter-Faith Council and the Hospital Auxiliary at North Carolina Memorial Hospital (now UNC Hospitals).

Dickie lived with them until her husband had a serious heart attack in 1969. Dickie then moved to the Murdoch Center in Butner, North Carolina. They were not physically able to lift a thirty-eight-year-old man anymore. "It nearly killed all of us when Dickie went to live in Butner," Thompson said. Dickie died two years later.

"Aunt Clemmie was grateful that Dickie didn't die before Uncle Bill did. She knew how painful it would have been for him. They really loved Dickie and treated him like he was normal—as much as possible," said Phillips.

In Thompson's room at Carol Woods are a few pieces of furniture and artwork from her lifetime of homes. On one wall hangs a caricature of her husband by cartoonist Jeff McNelly (and on the dresser is Bill's picture, looking very much like the drawing). "The people over at the *Chapel Hill Weekly* gave that to Bill. He and Orville were good friends; he'd go over to the paper every Saturday and sit around with the fellas." McNelly began his professional career at the newspaper before winning three Pulitzer Prizes, and Orville Campbell was once publisher and part owner of the *Weekly*, which has become the *Chapel Hill News*. The drawing has the inscription "Your cup is waiting…and so are all your friends at the *Weekly*," with about twenty signatures on it.

When Bill and Clemmie became Chapel Hill residents in 1923, they also became avid fans of the UNC basketball team and would walk to Woollen Gym for the games. She didn't get to attend a game in the Dean E. Smith Center until she turned 102 and the Carol Woods staff arranged for her to go and sit on the second floor in the handicapped section. According to a story in the *News & Observer*, Thompson greatly enjoyed the experience. "It was an honor for me," she was quoted as saying in the story. "We were treated like royalty." The royal treatment continued with a note from Tar Heel coach Dean Smith thanking her for her devotion. Later on, two players visited her during her half-year birthday party in July.

This gracious southern lady who outlived all her siblings, her husband and her two children and even a great-grandchild, who died after only sixteen days, had these parting words: "They have things to do here all the time, and some of my friends go to everything, but not me. I'm not going to wear myself out trying to do it all. I do the things I choose to do." Such are the words of wisdom from one who traveled a long road, choosing the right things for herself along the way until her death at age 104 on March 3, 2001.

Mack Foushee

Ask an African American Orange County native about his or her background and slavery will likely be part of the answer. Many surnames are those inherited from the white owners of their parents or grandparents. Mack Foushee, a dapper and lighthearted ninety-nine-year-old when interviewed in 2000, was the son of two former slaves. As a little boy, his father had been sold for fifty cents.

"For strong little boys, they'd give fifty cents," Foushee said. "If you looked like you might not make it, they'd give twenty-five cents." His father not only proved himself worth that half dollar, he also lived to the age of 103. But once freed, life changed little, according to his son. "He stayed on the white man's farm. The white man would say, 'You my nigger.' He was still considered the property of his owner. The big boys built a church and said, 'Let's get the slaves together.'"

Foushee explained that the former slaves, having known only what they had been exposed to on the property of their owners, remained dependent on the whites. The church was where they could go to meet others and where marriages could be arranged between the "owners" to determine where the couple would live. Instead of being paid wages, a house was built for them; they were fed and encouraged to reproduce. "It was awful, awful," Foushee said.

Such was the house where he was born, as one of five boys and five girls. "Sometimes big white guys would pull you away and take you to his farm and keep you hid. You wouldn't know where you were or how to get back. You had to keep your mouth closed to stay alive." It didn't take much to rub certain white men the wrong way, Foushee said, the result being that one was hanged from a tree or cut up. "Then they'd take a note and wrap it around a rock and throw it on the porch to tell you where to find your son," he said. When things went well, the family worked together in the tobacco fields on a piece of land in Bynum (ten miles south of Chapel Hill in Chatham County) that had been given to his father by his former owner. "We didn't see money working in the field but maybe got some new shoes," Foushee said.

He remembered his first outing to Chapel Hill at age twelve. He got jobs cutting grass through an older brother who lived on the Chatham/

Orange County line. "I got the taste of a little money. My brother had a nickel and I had a dime, but I wanted the nickel because it was biggest," he said as a smile spread across his face. He eventually learned the marble and tile trade and traveled the Southeast following jobs, sometimes even venturing as far as New York and Chicago. When he was close to age fifty, he helped build North Carolina Memorial Hospital.

The traveling kept him from settling down and marrying, but it didn't keep him from the ladies. "Every time I fell in love with a pretty one, I had to go to another town. I've never been married," Foushee said, pausing dramatically. "You'll never get to ninety-nine if you've got a wife—they'll kill you one way or another!" He held up his siblings as examples, as none of them had lived to his age. "They were all married," though his parents were clear exceptions—even his mother who bore ten children lived to eighty-nine.

When he could no longer handle the heavy lifting of his trade, he worked in home healthcare until age eighty-seven, cooking and providing for people during an illness or after a hospital stay so they didn't have to go into nursing homes. Foushee had recently moved into an apartment at Carolina Springs in Carrboro, where he frequently entertained friends when not joining them at the Northside Senior Center.

"He's the best host I've ever known," said George Parrish, fifty-five. "I've known him about all my life. He's a godfather to me, something special." Foushee had been friends with Parrish's father. "He always welcomes people to his house. His mind is real swift," Parrish said. "And he loves to get dressed. The first thing he does in the morning is start dressing. Even if he has no place to go, he gets dressed because if someone stops by wanting to take him somewhere, he doesn't want them to have to wait."

We had met at the Northside Senior Center, in the building where classes for African American children had been held. As we spoke, his friends gathered around to learn more about him. In excellent health, Foushee said that his only medication was for indigestion and heartburn. "But my doctor told me I was going to have to take something for love," Foushee said with a twinkle in his eye. With that, the group of friends gathered around "Papa Mack," as they called him, cracked up and one of them commented that he sure didn't need Viagra.

Though he chewed tobacco for a while and could often be found with a lollipop dangling from his mouth, Foushee was never a smoker. "I'm not a fussy eater," adding that he does his own cooking, eating mostly greens and meats. One of his friends mentioned sauerkraut, to which he said, "Oh, I love that."

When asked what one piece of advice he might give to young people, Foushee thought about it for a few minutes before saying, "Quit being so nobody can tell you nothing. Listen to your mama and daddy. You've got to let somebody tell you."

Keith Edwards, nutrition site manager at Northside Senior Center, appreciated the importance of the message. "If children of today were exposed to Mr. Mack and Miss Luella [the queen of the senior center—Luella Merritt, age ninety-four], I think they'd be better citizens because they'd have a full understanding of what it's like to be treated differently because of the color of their skin," Edwards said. "If these people can put what they've been through behind them and go on, then there's something seriously wrong when we cannot. They have lived our history—I've read about it in the history books, but they lived it and can talk about it."

Olivia Farrington Edwards

For as long as she could remember, Sarah Olivia Farrington Edwards, who went by Olivia, was referred to as "that old tall girl." At age ninety-five she still accepted the description, though in her mind she had always envisioned a different body type. "I always wanted to be short and fat, like a duck. A duck's feet are flat and their legs are short," she said from a chair in her comfortable, tidy Lindsay Street home. In her prime she stood close to six feet tall. She was easy to pick out in a photograph of three young women taken in the 1920s. Besides standing out as the tall one, she looked the same—as though she had hardly aged. Even her doctor had been taken by surprise when learning her age.

"He didn't believe it when I said I was born in 1904," Edwards said. She was born on an Orange County farm west of University Lake, the eleventh of twelve children born to free slaves. "I don't remember ever seeing my mother," she said. Her mother died while giving birth to her youngest brother. But that wasn't the end of having siblings. "My father had two sets of children," she said, explaining that he married again. "One was out and another was in," and he "had a bushel and a half" of offspring. Helping out on the farm kept her from attending school often, but she learned how to read and write. "I loved the farm, but I hated that cotton pickin'. I didn't mind chopping tobacco. What I enjoyed most was working with flowers in the garden," but that kind of gardening mostly came later in life.

In 1922, she married Henry Edwards, and they had four children, their firstborn son dying in infancy. When they moved to Chapel Hill in 1926, Henry, who died in 1975, continued working at a sawmill in the country, and Olivia's forty-year career at the university laundry facility began. She worked on the shirt line, where she touched up the pressed shirts of the young men. She said, "I worked on the chain gang. My nephew said, 'Forty years on the chain gang—that's too long to lay dead.'" Before the Great Depression, her wages were eight dollars and seventy-five cents per week, but the bad economy knocked it down to less than five dollars per week. "It was fifteen years before I got a paid vacation, and the only paid holidays we got were one day off for Thanksgiving and Christmas. I never made more than twenty-five dollars in a week." Summers were the hardest. "There weren't a lot of women in school and not a lot of men went to summer school," she said, and without enough shirts there wasn't enough work. Willing to do anything, "I'd wash windows or clean a floor, whatever needed to be done, for twenty-five cents an hour."

Her children and grandchildren called her Mama. "They say, 'Mama, I wouldn't work like that.' So I ask them, 'Where would you have worked?'" She helped them see how it was for her and tried to make it better for them when she started voting years earlier. "I voted to help people have things be better." She said she couldn't remember when she started voting but knew that it was decades earlier when a cousin ran for the school board. And though she had voted the previous week, she couldn't recall whom she had voted for. "I'd rather tell you I forgot than tell you a lie," she said. "My Daddy said there's no forgiving an uncalled-for lie."

Modest, matter-of-fact and with a keen sense of humor, Edwards kept asking why her story was worth writing. She neglected to mention the

Jefferson Award received in 1983 that was among family photos on a table along with the proclamation from then Chapel Hill mayor Joseph Nassif, who cited her for rendering "such labors of love as going into the homes of the sick, the aged, the needy, the forgotten and helping in whatever manner was needed by cleaning, cooking or nursing without any consideration for herself." Edwards held forth that it had cost her nothing to live that way, that what was important to her was having no regrets about things left undone—or things done that she shouldn't have. "I thank the Lord. He's been good to me," she said. A longtime member of First Baptist Church of Chapel Hill, she taught Sunday school many years and sang in the choir for fifty years. "I didn't know when I hit sixty I was gonna live to ninety-five. I feel satisfied all the way up."

She never drove a car and didn't like iced tea, and nothing of alcohol, tobacco or snuff ever passed her lips, but prolonged age brought an infected lung, a weak heart and knees and the need for a three-pronged cane. "I can't walk without holding this, but I thank the Lord I have this." She gave up her one admitted vice when she quit the laundry—drinking one Pepsi a day. "The Pepsi started working on my kidneys. I like to drink hot water." She continued to do her own cooking and cleaning. "My house ain't clean, but I try to keep the buzzards out," she said, laughing. Forced by the birds, Edwards's mornings started earlier than she preferred. "I wake up around six thirty or seven and listen to the birds. They start softly, seeming to say, 'Get up, get up'; then they're yelling, '*Get up*!' And I get up."

Quotes from her father peppered conversation. She said, "Daddy used to say, 'Don't ever take out the last egg in the hen house or they won't make no more.' You always want to leave a nest egg, sister." When a visitor commented that he hoped to still be kicking like she was when he reached her age, she responded, "Well, don't kick it all out now. Ain't nobody been no younger than I've been, but not many get older."

She died at age ninety-seven on August 2, 2002.

PART II

GETTING THINGS STARTED

If you're here for a few days, enjoy it! If you're here for a few years, make the most of it. If you plan to stay forever, help us to keep the spirit of the University and the community alive.

—Orville Campbell, editor and publisher of the Chapel Hill News, *1954–87*

Anyone tempted to believe that the summer season enticed the founders of the university as much as the place clearly has not lived in Chapel Hill over the course of a year. Of all the seasons, summer has the most to dread—not so much for the heat and humidity, with normal mean temperatures in the high seventies (only a handful of days each year break the one-hundred-degree mark)—but for the ticks, mosquitoes, chiggers and other small creatures that can make life difficult. Winter isn't so bad, with the coldest normal mean temperatures in January at forty degrees, though on January 17, 1977, it was negative one degrees Fahrenheit; and most years see several inches of snow. Nature explorers in Chapel Hill relish the winter, when the bare trees allow the forests to be seen—and seen through, creating wonderful times for exploring. It's hard to choose between the two most wondrous seasons; fetching as fall is with its palette of reds and yellows, the explosions in the spring truly bring the fever for everyone, starting slowly with the crocus and daffodils peeking up, sometimes through the last snowfall, followed soon after by forsythia, redbud and dogwood blooms. Add to that the efforts by generations of enthusiastic gardeners who have added their exotic mixes—magnolia trees, camellia and a profusion of azalea bushes—to the plethora of tantalizing native plants and you have a plant lover's paradise and a conclusion that there's no bad time to visit or live in Chapel Hill.

By the late 1920s, the Old Well on campus and other wells that had been drilled were strained to provide for the growing population, so a new source for drinking water was identified on approximately 210 acres of land a few miles southwest of the university, where three major streams—Morgan Creek, Price Creek and Neville Creek—could feed into it. A dam was built and University Lake was created in 1932. The university provided water and electricity to the community and in 1927 bought and managed the telephone system.

Newspapers had come and gone in the village, but when Louis Graves started the *Chapel Hill Weekly* in 1923, it stuck, and it continues several ownerships later as the *Chapel Hill News*. Graves was born (1883), bred and educated (UNC class of 1902 with a degree in French) in Chapel Hill, and Graves's father, Ralph H. Graves, had been a professor of engineering, mechanical arts, algebra and physics at UNC. His mother, Julia C. Hooper Graves, had been the daughter of UNC professor John Berniere Hooper, a descendant of William Hooper, a signer of the Declaration of Independence. Louis Graves, whose older brother Ralph introduced him to those he needed to know in publishing, had worked for the *New York Times* as a reporter and freelanced for several popular periodicals of the day: the *Saturday Evening Post*, the *Atlantic Monthly* and *Harper's*. In 1921, he started teaching journalism at UNC until he realized that his talents and the town would benefit more through service; so on March 1, 1923, he rolled out his first publication for the population of 1,700. The *Weekly* let people know what was happening in and out of town (those serving in wars or on trips) with the good villagers of Chapel Hill, and Graves remained more inclined to write about what was in bloom than about who had been arrested for whatever misdeed. He continued it for thirty-one years, including one extra year after selling it in 1954, when Orville Campbell took the reins for another thirty-three years.

Kiwanis Club

In 1928, as the automobile and other modern conveniences changed life, the formation of two civic clubs introduced a new form of fellowship to Chapel Hill. The businessmen of town would now have an umbrella under which to gather and focus attention on service to their community with either the Rotary Club or the Kiwanis Club. Frank Porter Graham, who would later lead the consolidated University of North Carolina system as its first president, was a professor of history at UNC–Chapel Hill when he helped charter the Kiwanis Club.

The Kiwanis Club celebrated seventy-five years of local service in 2003 with an anniversary party in the main room of the Chapel Hill Country Club. Sam Holton, who served as historian for the anniversary

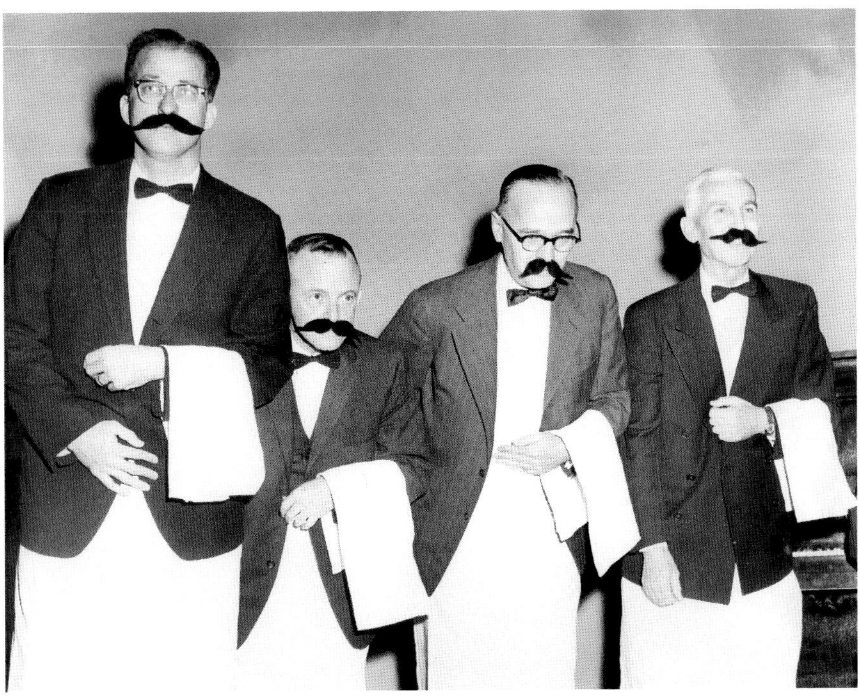

This photo had "Kiwanis Fun Night" written on the back and features, from left, Orville Campbell, editor and publisher of the *Chapel Hill News* from 1954 to 1987; unidentified; Temple Gobbel; and Carlyle Shepard. *Courtesy the Gobbel family.*

event, had been a Kiwanian for fifty years (only forty-eight years in Chapel Hill) and described the way it had been in the banquet program: "Seventy-five years ago Chapel Hill was a village of 2,500 people, a figure that had increased over the 1,495 reported in the 1920 census. The village community was contained on the hill." Franklin Street was "on the hill," and at that time only an eighteen-foot-wide swath in the 100 block of East Franklin Street was paved; the hitching posts and spaces for angle-parking vehicles remained dust bowls or mud pits at the whims of the weather.

On September 28, 1928, the *Chapel Hill Weekly* noted the chartering of the club in a front-page story. "About two hundred men and women, more than half of whom were visitors to the village, gathered at a dinner in the Baptist church social rooms Tuesday evening for the presentation of a charter to the Kiwanis Club of Chapel Hill." There were thirty-nine names on the charter. The list included well-known Chapel Hillians such as R.B. Fitch (Fitch Lumber), R.W. Foister (Foister's Camera Shop), R.L. Fowler (Fowler's Food Store), Georg Livas (Carolina Coffee Shop) and C.L. Martindale (Chapel Hill Airport manager). Included among the charter members were a cabinetmaker, heating engineer, plumber, circulation manager for the *Durham Morning Herald*, bank teller, operator of a print shop, two airplane pilots and manager of the railroad station. It would be 1974 before the first African American, Bill Thorpe, joined and 1987 before women were allowed to become members.

The club met at the Carolina Inn until about 1988, when it started meeting at the Chapel Hill Country Club. Until its peak in 1988, when membership totaled 158, it grew steadily. Seventy-five years after its beginning, however, membership had decreased steadily to 39 members, 61 percent of whom were retired. "There are two ways of looking at that," Holton explained at the banquet. "We're getting older. And the larger portion of our club are good Kiwanians who recognized a good club when they came to Chapel Hill and became members."

Detroit was where Kiwanis originated, in January 1915, as an opportunity for businessmen to gather and determine ways to give to the poor. It became an international organization in 1916 and by 1919 had developed its focus into service for children. The Durham club started in 1920 and helped with the founding of the Chapel Hill club. A table of

Durham Kiwanians at the anniversary celebration testified to the strong continuing ties between the clubs.

Bill Olsen, whose mother Sarah Olsen had been the first woman to become a real estate agent in Chapel Hill, remembered his first Kiwanis meeting, but it wasn't as an adult. "I came to a meeting in 1944 as a junior Kiwanian," he said. "I came to thank the club for donating uniforms to the Chapel Hill High School football team." A photo of a Kiwanis Fun Night from the late 1940s or early 1950s shows Kiwanians in different states of dress as football players, cheerleaders and such. "It was a wonderful mixture of rural and town/university people," Olsen said later of the club in the 1940s when his father was active. "They were the fathers of people I knew."

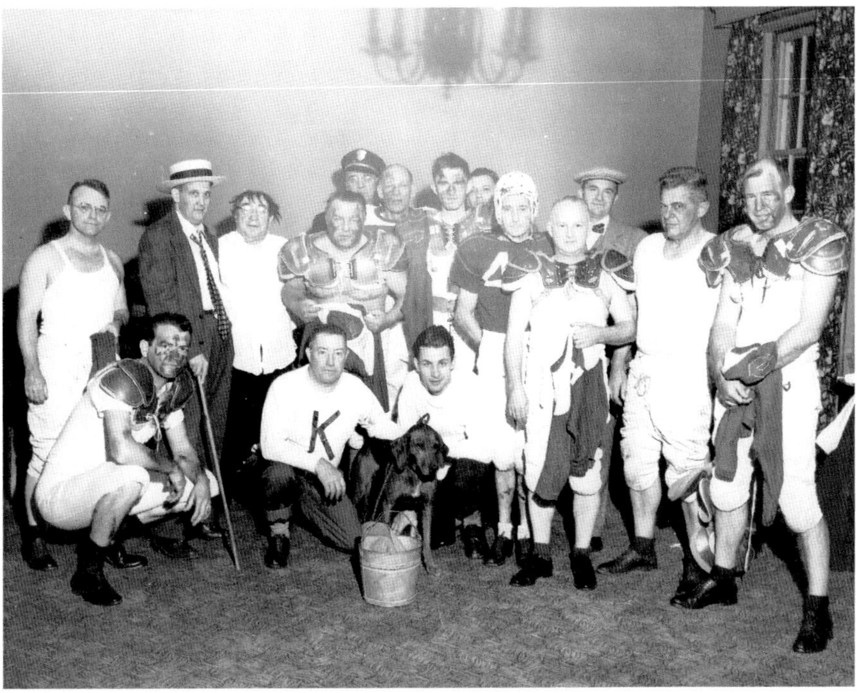

Wacky Kiwanians. Nobody claims to know anything about this photo from a meeting—obviously at the Carolina Inn and probably from the late 1940s or early 1950s—except that the man in partial football uniform kneeling on the far left looks like Bill Grice, who was the Chapel Hill High School football coach during those years. *Courtesy the Gobbel family.*

Kiwanis has had a continuing presence in Chapel Hill with its many fundraising and awareness-raising events over the years, from Fun Nights at the Carolina Inn in the 1940s to its annual Fourth of July fireworks displays at Kenan Stadium begun in 1954. "Several members at this time had served in the artillery and were adept at managing the mortars used to shoot off the more spectacular of the displays," Horton wrote. The shows continued, with home-grown James Taylor performing several years, until the stadium was expanded and the town took over the fireworks display. Kiwanis charged admission and concessions were sold, raising money for the programs supported by the club. Also in 1954, the club began its pancake breakfasts, which continue even still, though the venue has changed several times. When it began, under the presidency of Rogers Wade, breakfasts were held in the cafeteria of Chapel Hill High School, which was then located where University Square now exists. When the high school moved, the breakfast stayed downtown in the basement of University United Methodist Church, where it was for many years a highly anticipated community event.

Clarence Whitefield, a member since 1960, shared the history of the Terrific Kids program, which began in North Carolina in 1982. "It started in Black Mountain ten years before Kiwanis International adopted it as an international project," Whitefield said. "A teacher in Black Mountain said, 'I would not want to teach in a school that did not have a Terrific Kids program.'" In Glenwood Elementary School, the only school in town supported by the Terrific Kids program, there is a banner that says "This school is full of Terrific Kids." Kiwanis now also provides citizenship awards to middle school and high school students and $1,500 scholarships to each high school. In the early 1990s, Kiwanis made an extensive effort to construct and/or repair playgrounds at several elementary schools.

At the anniversary celebration, Mary Gavalas, the governor of the Carolinas District, said, "This club is one of the elders of Kiwanis. People like you make Kiwanis what it is today. This is the highlight of my year, being here to wish you well, wish you happy birthday," she said. "I want to thank each and every one of you for being Kiwanians."

Institute of Government: Albert and Gladys Coates

Chapel Hill offers several excellent examples of men who achieved greatness in no small part through the parallel efforts of their mates. Albert and Gladys Coates are one of several such couples included in this book.

Albert, from eastern North Carolina, graduated from UNC in 1918 before entering Harvard Law School, from which he received a degree in 1923. The two met while Gladys, a native of Portsmouth, Virginia, was a junior at Randolph-Macon Woman's College, where she received a degree in history in 1924 before spending the next four years teaching. Albert started teaching criminal law in the UNC law school in 1925, and in 1928, Gladys, then twenty-six, joined him in Chapel Hill as his bride. "Mr. Coates used to characterize their marriage by saying it was a match of Tidewater, Virginia, with Swampwater, North Carolina," said Henry Lewis, Kenan professor emeritus in the UNC School of Government.

Their union created a team that provided a force to be reckoned with for anyone standing in the way of their goal—an idea conceived the year they married and born in 1931—of an institute where students were taught how to govern, filling in the gap between textbook and application of laws in town halls, county courthouses and beyond. The Institute of Government was called a "boondoggle" by the chair of the law school. But Albert started teaching local officials in "schools" (perhaps today they would be called seminars) that he organized in which police officers, sheriffs and others could better understand implementation of their jobs.

Not even the Great Depression could defeat the young couple's determination, as Gladys studied the politics and leaders of various areas across the state and started mailing lists. The institute began as a private enterprise, with the pair nurturing it and those who attended it, and initiated the publication of *Popular Government*. With the dues provided by cities and counties it served, and using their own funds and donations from friends, its first headquarters opened on November 29, 1939, in a newly built colonial Georgian-style brick building at 223 East Franklin Street (on the site of the former Pickard Hotel, destroyed by fire in 1928).

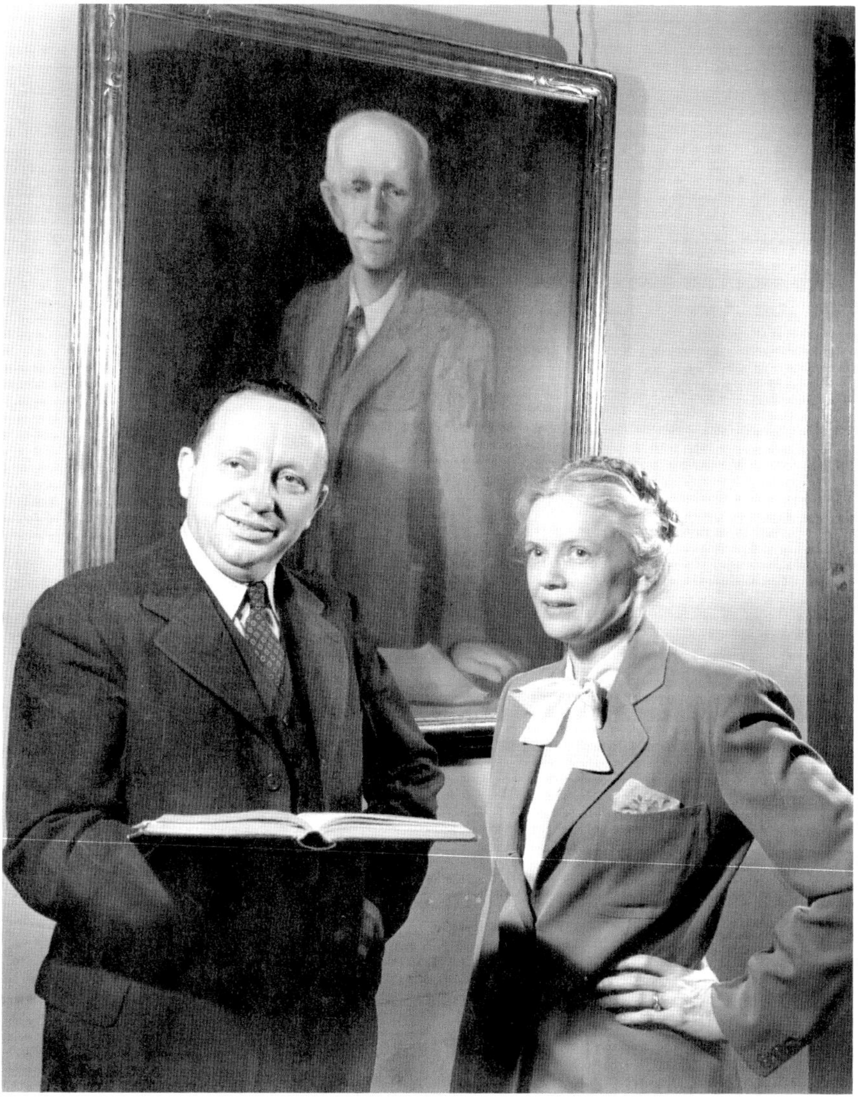

Albert and Gladys Coates with a portrait of Horace Williams looking over their shoulders. *Courtesy the UNC School of Government.*

It was the first such institute in the United States. Franklin D. Roosevelt commended it, saying, "I hope that states having no comparable agency will recognize and follow North Carolina's leadership." The institute became a part of the university in 1942, providing new stability with the support of state budgetary funds. Its programs expanded along with staff, and in 1956, the school moved into a new, larger facility on South Road named after the foundation that provided the funds, the Joseph Palmer Knapp Building.

With the institute and its students as their progeny, Albert was busy with the day-to-day business of running it while Gladys has been credited with managing it, plus running a household that could feed however many men her husband returned home with at the end of a day, hosting annual Christmas parties and handling any other event that the university required of her. She kept her mind busy as well, reading prodigiously, editing Albert's writing and doing research for dozens of books penned by Albert, including the one in 1975 titled *By Her Own Bootstraps: A Saga of Women in North Carolina*, which he dedicated to her, writing in part, "She has edited nearly everything I have ever written—cutting out purple passages, frying off fat, and adding insult to injury by improving the final product in ways which could not be denied." Albert retired in 1962, at a time when retirement was mandatory at age sixty-five. He died in 1989. In 1997, the Coates name was officially placed above the entrance of the institute's first building on Franklin Street. In 2001, the "Institute" became the "School" of Government.

When Gladys was ninety-five, the UNC Woman's Club learned at 3:30 p.m. on the afternoon before its annual spring luncheon at the Carolina Inn that their speaker would not be able to attend. Former governor Terry Sanford had died, and the scheduled speaker, Carmen Hooker, would be accompanying her husband, Chancellor Michael Hooker, to the funeral. The Woman's Club president, Joy Murphy, had heard Gladys Coates speak a few weeks earlier at the University Women's Center about the history of women at Carolina. "I knew that she was planning to attend the luncheon because she had said she was looking forward to hearing Carmen speak," Murphy said. When Murphy called Coates to ask if she would be willing to speak the next day, Coates said, "Give me thirty minutes to look at my notes to see if I can do it."

At the luncheon the next day, the fellowship between some two hundred women, the delicious food, the beautiful centerpieces and the presentation of the new officers were only a prelude to the interesting and rousing speech to follow. Jean Phay introduced Gladys Hall Coates with a description of her contributions to Chapel Hill and the university, saying, "As you know, Albert Coates founded the Institute of Government on this campus. Gladys was an essential part of that endeavor, from doing secretarial work to hostessing, to planning both buildings that housed that institution." Gladys was also fourth president of the University Woman's Club, was awarded an honorary professorship of public law and government at the institute and is an honorary member of the Order of the Golden Fleece and the Order of the Grail Valkyries, all of which Phay included in her introduction.

An overwhelmed Coates took her place at the podium, saying, "I don't know who I am. No one could live up to that!" Yet, only a handful of years away from a century of life, she stood there and did just that. She spoke of the debates that had begun in the early days of the nineteenth century: were women made only for procreation? Should women receive a liberal education? Is the female sex inferior in intellectual faculties to the male sex? Ought a female to hold the reins of any government?

"Women were so rare on campus in those days that when any were unexpectedly glimpsed, the cry would reverberate through the dormitories—'Angels on campus!'" And it was an important cry, she said, because men often walked back to their dorms from their baths in the basement of the library (now known as the Playmakers Theatre) clad in only a towel during warm weather. In 1877, UNC held its first summer school (the first university summer school in the nation), and of 235 students, 107 were women—the first breakthrough in education for women. Coates explained that in 1897, through the suggestion of university president Edwin Alderman, the doors were opened to women "to satisfy their demand and to carry gentle peace to silence envious tongues," as Coates quoted the then president. They were allowed to enter after graduating from a women's college, which in those days was a two-year program. Though the school's trustees agreed, some newspapers in the state were decidedly opposed. "'We are not Yankeeized enough in our ideas,'" Coates quoted one editor as writing, "'to accept this mixing of sexes in universities and colleges.' He favored a separate state university for women."

The women of the club listened with rapt attention as Coates moved through the strides that women have made, even though they had to do such things as wear hats and gloves to class in the early days. She had seen and been part of many changes. She quoted Frank Porter Graham (university president from 1930 to 1949) as saying, "I believe that education in a university is not a sex right but a human right… My belief in co-education at the university is a part of my belief in the university." Coates concluded her talk by sharing how thrilled she was with the appointment of Molly Corbett Broad as UNC system president in the same year as the 100th anniversary of "the coming of women to the University of North Carolina at Chapel Hill. May the next one hundred years of women on this campus be as fruitful as the first one-hundred years have been!" she said robustly.

When Gladys herself celebrated one hundred years in 2002, many people wanted to add their wishes to her in a *Chapel Hill News* story. Bob Anthony, curator of the North Carolina Collection in Wilson Library on the university campus, wrote:

> *We in the North Carolina Collection just adore her. She's a wonderful person. Mr. Coates used to come into the collection quite a bit, and I knew her through him first. She's one of the very few people still living who knew Thomas Wolfe personally. Wolfe was a roommate of Mr. Coates' at Harvard Law School.*
>
> *She worked on the history of the student government, creating a wonderful resource. When students come in looking for background on the university, it's the first thing we direct them to. I grew up in the eastern part of the state, and she had a friend in Tarboro. A couple of years ago, I'd take her with me when I'd go for a visit and drop her off at her friend's place. She would visit and I'd pick her up the next day on my way back. I was always amazed at how extensive and diverse her reading was. She was reading Hamilton's "Greek Mythology," the letters of Louis Brandeis, a biography of Eleanor Roosevelt and a book by a local novelist. She wouldn't mention the novelist by name but said, "She's good. She's done her best."*

> *She always liked learning and reading. She put me to shame at how much she read and retained. You could get her talking and she would go into a recitation of a poem.*

"When I came to the Institute of Government in March 1946, there was an absolute flood of veterans after the war," said Henry Lewis.

> *It looked like I was going to have a rough time finding a house. Mr. and Mrs. Coates took me into their house, and I lived there for a couple of weeks. I had come here to teach at the institute, which was their child. I was director of the institute for a while and one of the things I thought was important was to get a portrait of Mr. and Mrs. Coates together. Everybody agreed that it should be of both of them. We got a very fine painter to do it. I use that as an example of her devotion to the institute and her determination. It was a team effort. She was wonderful in giving annual Christmas parties for the staff and their families. That was always a great event. We would read poems and sing songs—these lovely parties were really extraordinarily nice.*

Elmer Oettinger, professor emeritus of public law and government and former assistant director of the Institute of Government, remembered Albert Coates from before his arrival in Chapel Hill:

> *My own recollections of this remarkable couple go back to 1930 when Albert was the speaker at my high school commencement exercises in Wilson and later the same year when the Coates' first invited me to dinner at their home in Chapel Hill. To my impressionable freshman ears, the dinner conversation had magic in its warmth and creativity as I learned of their mutual devotion and involvement in his plans for an Institute of Government translating "government in books" into "government in action" through teaching and training programs for state and local officials. Everyone knew Gladys complemented and furthered Albert's ideas with her own cogent thoughts and gracious personality. To appreciate Gladys Coates' 100 years is to provide some degree of belated recognition to an important achiever. A fascinating century of*

charming, constructive life, Gladys Coates leaves us all the better for her grace, style and accomplishments.

Even neighbors appreciated knowing the couple. "In the summer of 1985, my husband, Chris, and I moved to our current home on Hooper Lane with two teenage children in tow," said Caroline Martens, their next-door neighbor.

> *Albert Coates was the first neighbor to drop by. All four of us were invited to join the Coateses for dinner at the old Carolina Inn Circus Cafeteria. The only requirement was to spend an hour—almost to the minute—listening to stories about the Coates' years here in Chapel Hill and at the university. These stories were so closely shared by the couple that Albert would begin one and Gladys would complete it—likewise with many sentences. Our normally restless teens were fascinated. Chris and I were incredulous. Thus began a friendship that grew over the years. It was not until after Mr. Coates died in 1989, that I came to know her as the fiercely independent, politically liberal news junkie and bookworm that she really was. Never before had I enjoyed a close friendship with an octogenarian, let alone one who preferred CNN to the Movie Channel, the* New York Review of Books *to* Good Housekeeping *and double chocolate brownies to something more wholesome, like baked chicken, for dinner.*

"I spent time in their home as a child," said Chapel Hill lawyer Syd Alexander. "Early on, she was very clearly a strong advocate of women and would talk about the prominent role of women in the South. She was very deferential toward men but would not hesitate to hold up other women." As an adult, Alexander would sometimes use the provision of legal advice as a reason to visit her. "She would always serve tea and in conversation, jump from Homer to Chaucer to Shakespeare and it was all connected. She's had the ability to change with society like all bright, articulate, thinking people."

Bob Epting, another Chapel Hill lawyer, said that he owed his law degree to the couple. "Because of the work Gladys did alongside Albert, the Institute of Government hired me to teach in its highway patrol school while I was going to law school at Carolina and thus financed the legal education I would not otherwise have been able to afford," Epting said. "When I reminded him of this a year or so before his death, Mr. Coates told me I had earned my way, and would always be one of his and Gladys' boys."

William C. Friday, president emeritus of the university, brought together all her facets when he said:

> *Ida and I have known this gracious lady and wonderful neighbor for years, through dinner visits, sidewalk visits and book visits, she was always gracious and charming. She was the hostess, really, of the university.*
>
> *She was a necessary companion to Albert Coates. He could not have done it without her. She is the epitome of graciousness and what is known as the southern lady—gracious, gentle, vivacious and smart as the dickens! She's a very lovely person.*

Gladys Coates lived in the home that she and Albert had constructed via architect brothers John and James Webb in 1952 until her death at age one hundred on September 25, 2002.

NORTH CAROLINA SYMPHONY: BENJAMIN AND MAXINE SWALIN

By the standards of the day, Benjamin and Maxine Swalin (pronounced swah-LEEN) were no spring chickens when they arrived in Chapel Hill in the summer of 1935, after having married on New Year's Day in Missouri. Thirty-four and thirty-two, respectively, he from Minnesota and she from Iowa, both with training in and a passion for classical music, they were only beginning to get their feet wet as a couple, with the expectation of being here no longer than the late summer session, which Benjamin would teach in the music department. Before they knew it, the offer of a permanent position coupled with the allure of resurrecting an abandoned symphony would root them in as deeply as the trees that towered wherever they looked. The heat may have been "blistering," as

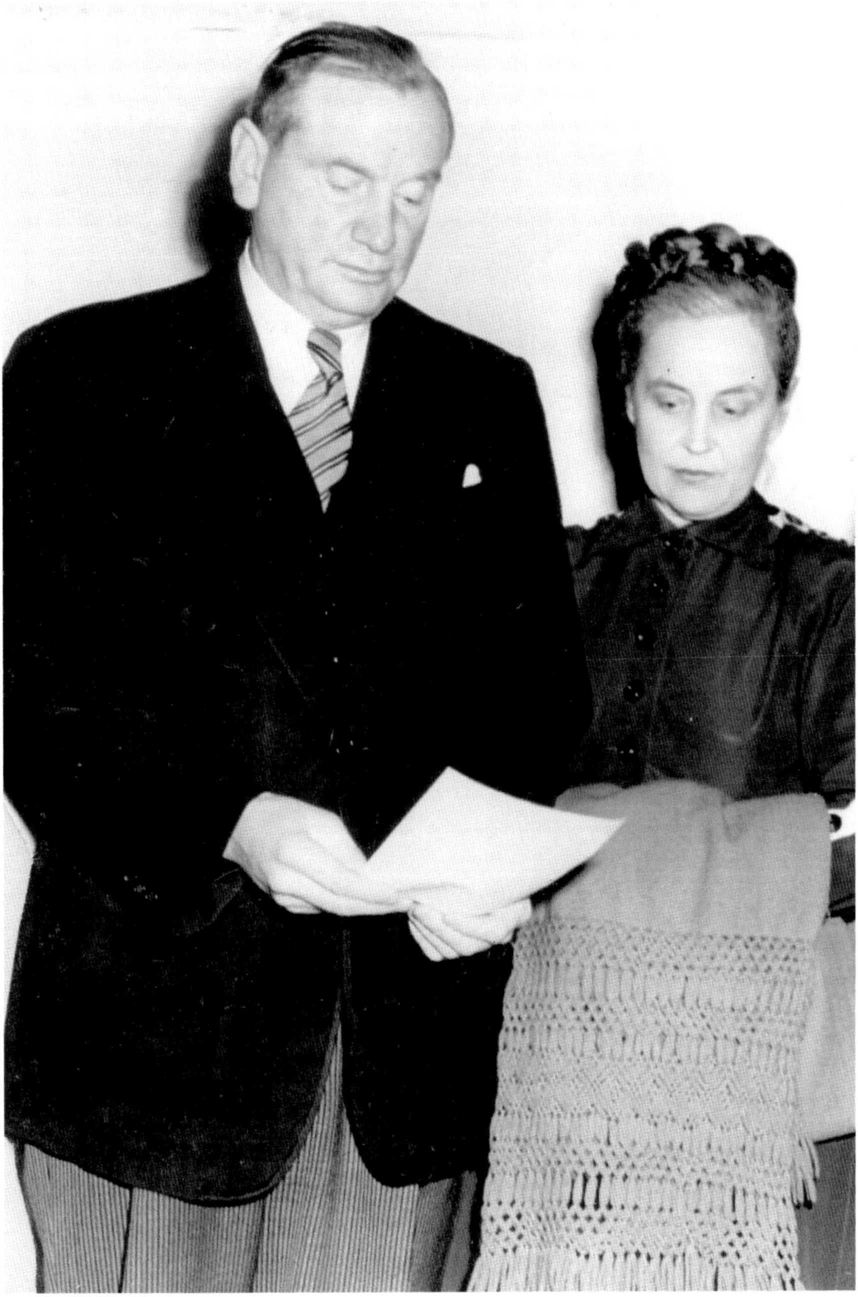

Benjamin and Maxine Swalin before enjoying, rather than performing, a concert, circa 1950s. *Courtesy Maxine Swalin.*

Maxine later described it, but too much promise presented itself during the six-week-long visit before Benjamin was to resume his position at DePauw University in Indiana. They had discovered talented people thirsty for musical leadership during their first evening when they met Paul Green, Johnsie Burnham and Adeline and Freddie McCall.

Paul Green, from Harnett County, North Carolina, taught philosophy and drama at UNC, and in 1927, he had won the Pulitzer Prize for drama for writing *In Abraham's Bosom*, a Broadway play dealing seriously with the plight of the American Negro in the South. Green was also a musician and in 1937 would write *The Lost Colony*, named as a forerunner to the American musical as the first and longest-running historical outdoor drama, which continues summer-long runs near the site of the events depicted in it, on Roanoke Island, North Carolina. He had learned about the Swalins from Dr. Glen Haydon, head of the music division at UNC, who was lending the couple his home when he and his family left for vacation.

Green called the Swalins after they arrived at the Carolina Inn and invited them out to meet some people. He took them to the home of Johnsie Burnham, who had been one of the first female violinists with the Metropolitan Opera Orchestra in New York. She had returned to her native North Carolina and settled in Chapel Hill after becoming a widow only five years prior at age forty-eight. She lived to age ninety-eight and was laid to rest next to her husband in 1980 in the Old Chapel Hill Cemetery, where the inscription below her name reads "She loved good music as she loved life itself." At her home, the Swalins also met Adeline and Freddie McCall. Adeline McCall, a music educator, would become invaluable to the couple, who instantly felt comfortable despite the assault from heat, humidity and, no doubt, claustrophobia from the riot of trees.

As Maxine said during the speech she gave on her 100th birthday as she received the 2003 North Caroliniana Society Award: "Never had we had such a good time!" This first evening in Chapel Hill introduced the Swalins to their destiny. "They told us that there had been a North Carolina Symphony, but, after about 140 concerts and a warm reception, the WPA [Works Progress Administration] had withdrawn its financial support. The requiem of an orchestra! 'How tragic,' we thought, little guessing that we would become instruments of its revival."

When Frank Porter Graham, then president of UNC, offered Benjamin a permanent position at the end of the session, the couple had made enough friends and felt comfortable enough with the political climate that they accepted the offer, even though it was for less money and more work. They had seen enough to believe that despite a dearth of musical education, North Carolina was ready for musical growth. Ben had studied in New York, Vienna and Moscow and had seen the positive results that a musical culture could bring to a society—so they started scouring the woods looking for musicians.

The decision to stay in Chapel Hill derailed Maxine's plan to pursue a master's degree at the University of Indiana, but Benjamin convinced her that she needed an advanced degree to be protected, according to Maxine, so she went to Cambridge, Massachusetts, to get her master's in the arts from Radcliffe. She had previously received a diploma in piano and theory from the Institute of Musical Art (Juilliard), where she met Benjamin, and a bachelor's at the University of Iowa. "He sacrificed willingly and we were separated for one year," she said. "It was a difficult year." Benjamin had studied with violin master Franz Kneisel at Juilliard and received bachelor's and master's degrees from Columbia University, as well as his doctorate from the University of Vienna; he knew about being separated from family during times of study.

Upon her return, acquiring a suitable place to live posed additional difficulty. While renting a small apartment next to University Presbyterian Church, she searched the town for larger, yet affordable, accommodations, even taking the suggestions of new friends to talk to people in their yards as she walked along streets. One day a young dentist she spoke to pointed to his mother's house behind his backyard and perhaps saw in Swalin an answer to his own dilemma of trying to get his mother, who was past being able to live safely on her own, to move into his home.

In her book *An Ear to Myself*, Swalin wrote:

> *That was my cue. After several "chance" exchanges with his mother who was tending her flowers at 303 N. Columbia St., I mentioned knowing her son. "He wants me to move in with his family," she said. "But I'll never give up this house."*

Not long after, the dentist called saying that his mother wondered if the Swalins would like to rent her house. When Maxine said that they would need a furnished house, he explained that his mother had fallen and would not be able to take anything with her, providing the couple with a house one block away from the center of Chapel Hill and a short walk to Benjamin's work on campus.

The house, which they later bought, sits across the street from where the first Chapel Hill fire station was later built, but at that time there was just a hill on which sat Mrs. Durham's house and barn, where she raised her children and kept a cow. After spending the summer of 1937 in New Hampshire, where Benjamin had been awarded a residency, the couple returned home to find that bulldozers had devoured the hill where Mrs. Durham and her children had lived, and the house was being moved into the empty lot next to theirs. Swalin wrote, "'We're opening an Airport road,' a State Highway official told us." Airport Road, which converged with Columbia Street just past their house, became the Chapel Hill portion of NC 86, a major entrance into Chapel Hill from Hillsborough to the north, connecting past the campus to 15-501, the road to Pittsboro to the south. It was renamed Martin Luther King Jr. Road in 2005 but retains mention as "Historic Airport Road" on street signs.

Maxine taught at Chapel Hill High School on South Columbia Street for one year before it burned down in 1942. That year of teaching music is what led to my introduction to Maxine when she was a mere ninety-four, at a Chapel Hill High School reunion in January 1998, ten years after the death of her beloved Benjamin. "The North Carolina Symphony started in 1932 but it was abandoned during government conflicts after three years. When my husband came here in 1935, a man would be humiliated to carry a violin across campus," Swalin said. "Little did we know there would be a North Carolina Symphony and I would be thirty-two years on tour with it." They traveled from late January through May to schools all over the state, playing for schools, introducing children and adults to classical sounds and influencing children to develop their musical abilities. "Now there are orchestras in high schools feeding into the wonderful stimulus of music," she said.

From the accomplished side of this mission, she made it sound easy, but many hurdles, including raising funds, had to be overcome before the real work could begin. Money was tight, and many others were asking for it to fund their dreams—like an institute of government or state hospital; where could money be found for something as ethereal as music? But through perseverance, the symphony was restarted through Benjamin's efforts in 1939, and its first concert was held on March 16, 1940, at Meredith College in Raleigh. Unfortunately, few bothered to attend. "Nancy Johnson of Raleigh wrote an article in the Raleigh paper [the *News & Observer*], scolding people for not attending the concert and supporting a movement that could develop into something important," Maxine said. The Swalins met with Johnson and shared their vision of a traveling orchestra that would take programs to people around the state, becoming part of an education process. Johnson excused herself, made a phone call and returned to the Swalins with an invitation to visit Governor Joseph Broughton and his wife at the Governor's Mansion. They did, and that discussion led Mrs. Broughton into action, and within a week a bill was introduced to the legislature in Raleigh to support a state symphony that would become part of the educational system. The "Horn Tootin' Bill" was passed in 1943, making North Carolina the first state to recognize the importance of an orchestra in its schools.

Eight years after moving to Chapel Hill, the long prelude finally segued into the composition that would become their opus. They began the complex task of annually taking the music, along with some fifty-five musicians and their instruments, both great and small, into all one hundred counties of a state where many still lived in great deprivation in a time when roads were not always paved, toilets were not always indoors and central heating and air conditioning were yet to be introduced—this all while Ben continued teaching classes at the university and rehearsing the orchestra in various places throughout the state on weekends. Yet, in its second tour season during the 1947–48 school year, the North Carolina Symphony played concerts for 100,000 children in the Old North State, with Benjamin conducting and Maxine playing the celesta, harpsichord or piano. At one concert in a school gymnasium so cramped for space that children sat at the musicians' feet, Maxine remembered a little boy saying to her after the concert, "Maybe I thought I just wanted to get out of class, but I enjoyed it very much."

The other chord that the symphony's visits always struck was the educational component, where Adeline McCall reenters the picture. The Children's Concert Division of the symphony was organized in 1945 with McCall as education director and Maxine as coordinator for the symphony and state elementary schools. Starting in 1950 and running through 1973, McCall wrote a run of *Symphony Stories* for the children's concert division.

At Maxine's 100th birthday celebration, many in attendance still remembered the magical feelings of attending the concerts, either as children or adults. "I was an elementary school child, and I remember going to concerts in Greensboro," said Barbara Parramore of Raleigh, who grew up in Guilford County. "We were exposed to music because of the symphony." "The Typewriter Song" remains a delightful memory for Parramore, who became a music educator and elementary school principal, seeing firsthand the results of the education program led by Adeline McCall.

Robert and Pearl Seymour met the Swalins soon after moving to Chapel Hill in 1959, when Bob became pastor of Binkley Memorial Baptist Church. "I always remember hearing her play the celesta in the orchestra," Pearl said, describing the hanging instrument with its sparking bell-like sound. "I always associate the symphony with her," said Pearl, who for years was the church organist.

H.G. Jones, secretary of the North Caroliniana Society—which was started in 1976 as a way to recognize an individual or organization for long and distinguished service in the encouragement, production, enhancement, promotion and preservation of the history, literature and/or culture of North Carolina—served as master of ceremonies at the birthday event. He spoke of the Swalins, saying, "Unlike so many people who come to view Chapel Hill as a way station on their way to somewhere else, they came and, within a few months, knew they were going to stay. They went to every corner of the state and took good music to people who hadn't heard it before," Jones said, pointing out that when they arrived, many people in the state didn't have radios. "They just fell in love with the state—and the state with them."

"When we feel at home outside of where we're born, that's where we're meant to be," Maxine said in her twenty-five-minute speech, which concluded with a standing ovation. A bouquet of flowers and a cake with three lit numerals (1-0-0) materialized, and Maxine's good friend John Lambert started singing "Happy Birthday" with everyone chiming in. Gracious, charming, composed and as radiant as ever in the glow of her candles, she blew them out and stood still for another serenade as Willis Whichard led everyone in singing the tune "Goodnight Irene"—but switching the name to Maxine.

Maxine did not consider her work done upon reaching the century mark. The university had started a new project called the Arts Common, where students of music and art could share space in a wedding of their talents, and she supported the endeavor by inviting people to her home to learn about it, enticing them with a concert of her impeccable piano artistry. In 2008, a group of her friends headed by Betsy Green Moyer, a daughter of Paul and Elizabeth Green, organized a fundraising concert in Memorial Hall starring two talented grandchildren of Paul and Elizabeth's—cellist Nancy Green, daughter of Paul Green Jr., and pianist Frederick Moyer, son of Betsy, on the occasion of Maxine's 105th birthday. With the money raised from the concert, a bench—one of the first two of the Arts Common—was purchased bearing a plaque honoring her as the "Grande Dame of the North Carolina Symphony," which was presented to her in honor of her 106th birthday. Maxine continues to live in her Chapel Hill home, seeking always the messages within good music, art and literature, continuing her remaining years without Benjamin as he had taught her: "Study—improve your mind—share your knowledge so it will help someone—keep your friendships in repair—think and act in Minuet time."

North Carolina Memorial Hospital: Reece and Norma Berryhill

The North Carolina Memorial Hospital
To serve as a continuing memorial to those North Carolinians
who have given their lives, and who may hereafter give their lives,
as members of the Armed Forces, in protecting the freedom and
common welfare of their fellow citizens.
—a plaque at the entrance to Memorial Hospital

Walter Reece Berryhill, the eldest of two living boys who grew up on a farm in Mecklenburg County, went to school in Chapel Hill in 1917 with the intention of becoming a minister. In 1919, he went to a football game in Raleigh and afterward met Norma Connell, the third of nine surviving children raised on a farm in Warren County, then a student at Peace College. Friendship emerged immediately but romance waited—both had aspirations beyond affairs of the heart. Reece, who was president of his class and a member of Di Society and Phi Beta Kappa, graduated in 1921, but the influenza pandemic of 1918–19 had changed his direction. His pursuit would be medicine; however, he had an obligation to fulfill back home. He had been given free tuition in exchange for at least two years of teaching, so he entered the field of education, first as an assistant supervisor at a private preparatory school in Charlotte and then as principal of Big Springs High School in the Queen City, both experiences providing further preparation for his future.

The year 1923 saw both Reece and Norma in Chapel Hill as he entered medical school and Norma, having received her associate's degree and having taught for a year in Norlina, entered UNC on full scholarship under the tutelage of Dr. Howard Odum, renowned for his research addressing regional and racial sociology and his expansion of roles for women on campus. After Reece completed the two-year medical program in Chapel Hill, he went to Harvard for years three and four. Norma received a bachelor's degree in sociology in 1925 and became director of the Girl's Club in Leaksville-Spray, now called Eden. She was offered a position as dean of girls at Charlotte's Central High School if she first completed the counseling and guidance program at Columbia University, so she moved to New York City and supported herself working with immigrant women in a settlement house there. She returned to Charlotte a year later and served three years as dean of girls at the high school. On the day that she married Reece in August 1930, almost eleven years after meeting, they moved to Cleveland, Ohio, where Reece was chief resident and for two years an instructor of medicine at Western Reserve College (now Case Western Reserve University).

With the promise of expansion of the medical school into a four-year program, the couple and their baby, Jane, returned to Chapel Hill in 1933, and Dr. Berryhill accepted the position of chief physician at the student infirmary. Their daughter, Catherine ("Cat"), was born, and Reece rose through the ranks until, in 1941, at the age of forty-one, he was named (the youngest) dean of the medical school, which was still a two-year program. It was the first medical school in the Old North State, started in 1879 about a decade after the end of the Civil War to prepare students for programs offered in leading medical schools, but his greatest longing was for it to provide full training for doctors.

Another war—World War II—provided a shameful statistic and the impetus to build a state hospital. During the war, no other state had more young men rejected for military service for health reasons than North Carolina. Its number of doctors and hospitals also ranked near the bottom. Not surprisingly, it ranked near the top in infant and childbirth deaths. In July 1945, the Medical Care Commission began its work of studying the health needs of North Carolina residents. For Reece Berryhill, dean of the School of Medicine at UNC, opening a hospital in Chapel Hill was imperative. But eight other cities wanted the hospital as well, and three of them—Charlotte, Greensboro and Raleigh, with larger populations—presented strong cases. Out-of-state consultants, however, saw the logic in having the hospital on the centralized campus of UNC–Chapel Hill and, what Berryhill had long anticipated, expanding the medical school into a four-year program.

"If you build a professional school on an outstanding university campus, you have a chance for it to be outstanding," said Christopher C. Fordham III, dean emeritus and UNC–CH chancellor emeritus, in 2002 on the occasion of the fiftieth anniversary of the hospital. "The interaction with the humanities, the social sciences and the arts has been very enriching to the medical school and, from the beginning, has helped draw excellent faculty."

On April 1, 1947, a legislative act created North Carolina Memorial Hospital. As a devoted and vocal member of the commission, Berryhill recommended a grassroots effort for raising awareness and funds, called "the Good Health Plan." Kay Kyser, who was still living in California, got into the act when he learned of the plan. He had learned the ropes about reaching large audiences during public service campaigns while helping raise money to increase the size and scope of Santa Monica, California's St. John's Hospital. So Kyser began employing the same

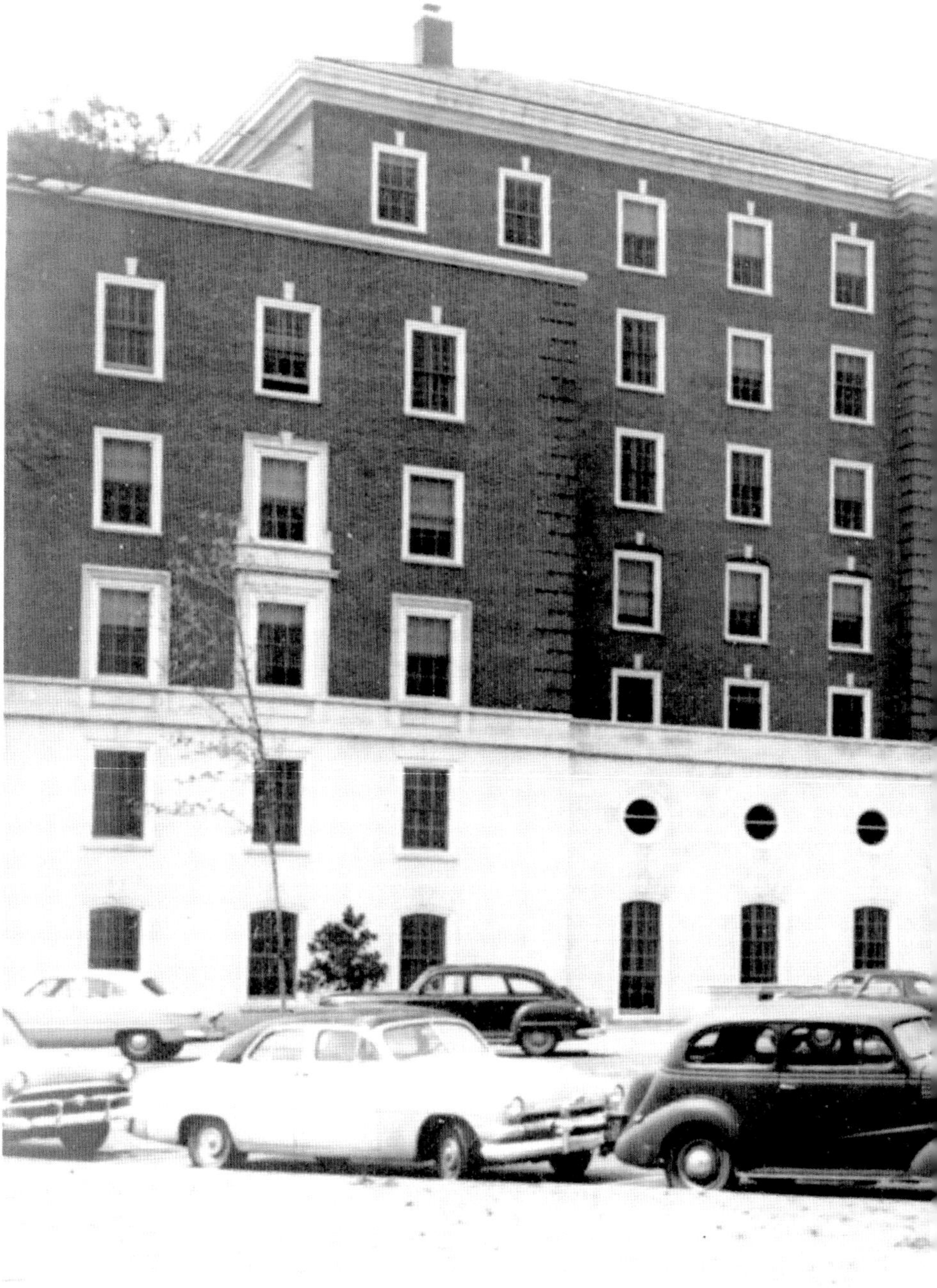

North Carolina Memorial Hospital shortly after opening in 1952. *Courtesy UNC Hospitals.*

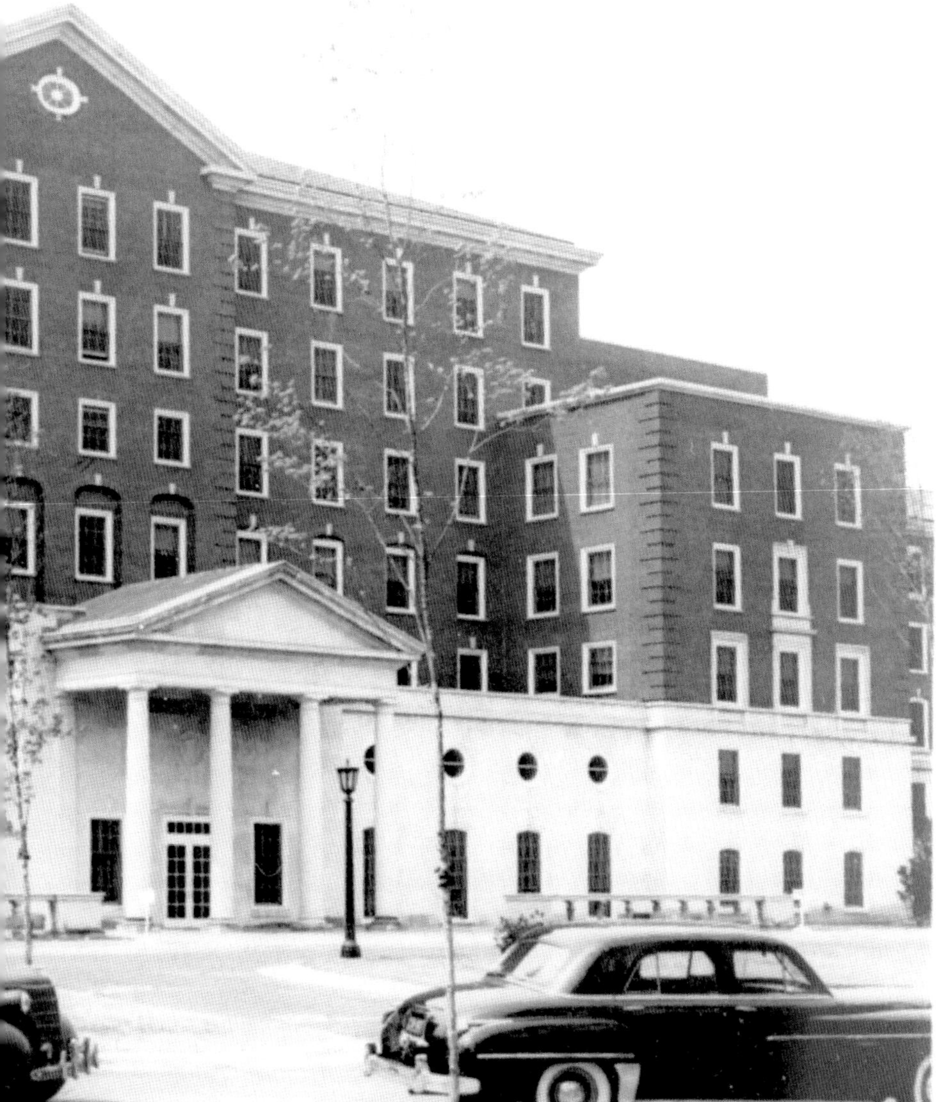

methods using his Hollywood resources. Songwriters Sammy Cahn and Jule Styne produced a song called "It's All Up to You," and Kyser got Frank Sinatra and Dinah Shore to sing it. On radios across his home state people heard:

We need vitamins and medicines and beds to spare
Places where the sick can go to get some care
Lots of new equipment to combat disease
Clinics where the poor can go for moderate fees…
If we do these things then we will be the state
Where the weak grow strong and the strong grow great.

In a then remote area near the southern edge of the campus, a portion of woods was cleared, and on October 11, 1949, ground was broken for the hospital. Eleven months later, the first director, Robert Cadmus, began tackling the problems of planning, construction, supply, personnel and organization. Berryhill proved a masterful recruiter as he lined up nationally prominent doctors for the school's new clinical departments.

Opening for business as North Carolina Memorial Hospital on September 2, 1952, only 250 of the 400 proposed beds were ready for use by the people of the state; there was a staff of 108 (not counting doctors); not all of the seven floors were finished; and the kitchen pantry held one hundred pounds of beans. "Meals came from the Carolina Inn for a while," said Wallace Womble, a long-retired supervisor in the purchasing department. "It wasn't long before we had food there."

The seventh floor had been completed first, and it was there that boxes of supplies were taken from their holding areas all over campus, according to Womble. Ordered supplies as well as gifts had been coming for years, and the Tin Can (where Fetzer Gymnasium is today), a corrugated tin structure the size of five basketball courts, which had served as the university's gym and dance hall, was stacked to the rafters with equipment. Supplies were located in dormitory basements, in any empty closet and also at Camp Butner in Durham.

The process of moving the equipment into the hospital became known as Operation Tin Can and required quite a feat. Throughout the summer, starting in June, boxes were moved into the hospital, where the

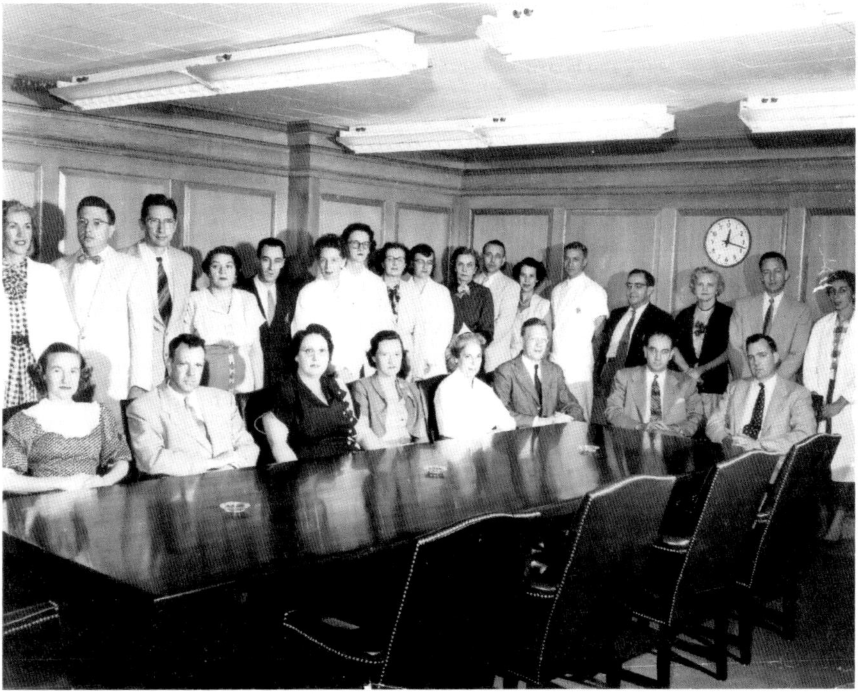

First department heads of North Carolina Memorial Hospital in 1952. *Back row, left to right*: Anne Ball, Wallace Womble, Ottaway Brown, Miss Sizemore, H.E. Thomspon, unknown, unknown, unknown, Margaret Moore, Viola Jacobs, Leon King, unknown, Bill Taylor, Mr. Ingram, Mrs. Thompson, Tom Peyton and unknown. *Seated, left to right*: Rachel Long, Frank Zinneman, Gladys Kohn, Annie Anderson, Miss Spaulding, Joe Greer, Dr. Cadmus and Gene Crawford. *Courtesy Wallace Womble.*

box openings made it feel like Christmas but the lack of air conditioning at the time made that particularly hot summer seem more like hell. "We would wet hankies and put them over our noses and mouths to go in and grab equipment," Womble said of entering the Tin Can. He said that pretty much every able-bodied male in town was roped into the activity that required fourteen- to sixteen-hour days for several months, the process aggravated by the discovery of a lack of compliance with strict instructions to label every box as it had arrived. "Sometimes the nurses didn't know what the equipment was, and we had to bring in catalogues to figure it out."

Of the gifts, one in particular had to be returned. "Dell Norfleet gave us a Hubbard tank," Womble said. The Hubbard wading hydrotherapy tank for the physical therapy department would not fit through the hospital doors. "We had to ship it back and later receive the replacement in two sections, which were welded together in its permanent location," Womble said. Margaret Moore, the hospital's first director of physical therapy, remembered it. "It was a beautiful instrument with a stretcher on it to put patients in. My first patient was a resident in OB/GYN who sprained his back getting furniture into his apartment." That resident was among sixteen interns and thirty-two residents who constituted the first class of physicians in the new four-year medical school in Chapel Hill. Moore, who was born and raised in Greensboro, had been living and working in New York City when she first heard about the hospital being built in Chapel Hill. She heard Dr. Berryhill speak at a seminar she was attending in Chicago. "Dean Berryhill said the medical school was being expanded, and a hospital was being built next to the medical school," Moore said. "I was startled at the news." Her desire to be part of the physical therapy department was so great that she wrote Berryhill a letter. "They flew me down," and she started work on April 1, 1952. "I was the eleventh person on the payroll."

In a photo taken from the air at that time, North Carolina Memorial Hospital was surrounded by forest, with the main entrance facing the campus that is nowhere in sight—on the opposite side from today's hospital entrance (moved around in 1969). What is not so clear from that photo is the significance of a second front entrance—the one for blacks, or the "colored."

"I had not seen anything like it," Elaine Hill said of segregation. She was from New York, and her husband, Dr. John Hill, had been recruited for the new hospital. "I didn't want to come. I never thought I'd leave New York." But rather than sit and pout, she became a volunteer at the hospital even before the first day, along with about 125 other local women volunteers. She went on staff at the hospital as director of volunteer services in 1967.

Christine Jones started work on August 15, 1952, as a nurse's aide. She said that segregation was a way of life for blacks at that time. "There were things for whites and things for colored," Jones said, and having experienced them, listed the demarcations: drinking fountains, waiting rooms, bathrooms, cafeterias and, of course, patient rooms and wards.

"The white cafeteria was on the first floor, the colored cafeteria was in the basement. The hospital was segregated for the patients, but the personnel was integrated." Concurring with what others had said, she spoke of the staff as one big happy family in which blacks were included—but with differences. "Blacks were called by their first name; handles (Miss, Mrs., Mr. and Dr.) were put on the whites."

One of the "firsts" at the hospital was the intensive care unit (ICU), started by Ethel Harrison, a nurse who used her common sense to begin a system for the sickest patients to get the greatest care. "Ethel Harrison was one of the most unique nurses who walked this planet," Moore said. "We were not supposed to mix whites and blacks," said Cookie Wilson, who joined the staff in 1958 and is credited with integrating the ICU. "If we had three white patients in a room with an empty bed, we couldn't put a black patient in there. We had to move patients from one room to another to keep the races separate." Besides creating additional work for the nurses, it could compromise patient care. "It was ridiculous," said Wilson, who would become head nurse of the ICU. "So, I did not move them." When asked if anyone complained, she chuckled and said, "Nobody opened their mouth."

Audrey Booth, who became director of pediatrics in May 1954, said that segregation wasn't much of an issue in pediatrics. "It made less of a difference to our patients," she said. Her most vivid memory of those days was during Hurricane Hazel, about a year after the hospital opened. "We lost all power," Booth said. "Pediatrics was on the seventh floor, and we had to carry everything up and down the steps. It was the time of the great polio epidemic, and the polio ward was my responsibility." There had been a polio epidemic on campus shortly after the opening of the hospital. "Polio hit the campus where the athletes ate," said Margaret Moore. "Ten or twelve athletes came down with polio." As a result, Moore had hired four physical therapists by Thanksgiving of the first year.

June Watson, who had worked as a public health nurse in Baltimore, came to work in the outpatient department one year after the hospital opened. She was from Kingston, New York, and had received an undergraduate degree from UNC after serving in the U.S. Army. She then received a master's degree from Columbia University. Still, she had never heard such accents before beginning her public health work at Memorial, where people from all over the state went for treatment. "People came from the country. Some of them had never been to a doctor before," Watson said. She said that for one dollar people could have a complete physical—once the nurses learned how to keep them there. "We'd send them down to X-ray, where they would be told to 'take a deep breath, hold it, OK, finished'—and they would leave. We didn't know what was happening." The patients didn't realize that there was more to the exam after the X-ray and never came back. As times changed, new methods developed.

"To a greater degree than most other medical schools around the country, ours has always been committed ideologically to improving the health of our state," said Jeffrey Houpt, dean of the School of Medicine and CEO of the UNC Health Care system in 2002. "There is a tradition here of looking at what the larger needs of the state are and making sure we address those in the very best way, whether through education, research or patient care." The school certainly made itself available, providing service for any state resident, including the only specialized burn-care facility—the North Carolina Jaycee Burn Center, named after the civic club that in 1973 started selling jars of jelly until earning $150,000 to help fund the unit. The Jaycees statewide have raised approximately $100,000 each year since. For Tar Heels who get into trouble in remote areas, UNC Hospitals has Air Care, an air ambulance service that transports more than one thousand patients a year to the hospital. And it has AHEC, the Area Health Education Centers program, which flies healthcare professionals out into the farthest reaches of the state to improve the health of North Carolinians.

"AHEC has done a great deal to create a better distribution of physicians and other healthcare professionals into rural communities, making services of quality more available to everybody in the state," said Glenn Wilson, who in 1972 became AHEC's founding director. "We have provided medical education to many more North Carolinians than we could have without AHEC, and the program has helped doctors and hospitals around the state provide more and better patient services."

Under the leadership of Berryhill-appointed George Hamm, the first chair of the department of psychiatry, UNC has led the way in integrating both psychological and biological approaches to mental illness. "What made him a heretic to some of his colleagues was his radical, rebellious notion that biology was also important," said Robert Golden, the department's chair in 2002. "Today, it's a given. But back then it was enough to get you burned at the stake."

The hospital complex has continued to grow, opening the North Carolina Children's Hospital and North Carolina Women's Hospital—the only ones in North Carolina to offer complete inpatient and outpatient care for women and children in one place. "These two new hospitals are a dream come true for many people because they so dramatically increase our ability to care for the women and children of North Carolina," said Eric Munson, president and chief executive officer of UNC Hospitals in 2002. "The clinical facilities with their cutting-edge technology are superb, but I am most excited about the warm, welcoming spaces like the pediatric playroom, Women's Resource Center and spacious public areas, all of which will help people feel better emotionally while they are here," Munson said.

More construction provides evidence that UNC Hospitals continues to expand its facilities and services and will, no doubt, be a vastly different place in another fifty years—like the transformation from its ambitious but more modest beginnings; but at least one thing will not have changed: the fact that the hospital continues to change as technology and practices advance.

Christine Jones worked there for more than thirty-two years. "The entire time I worked there, something else was being built," Jones said. "When they dug the hole, it started," Wallace Womble said.

Dr. Berryhill's work started it all, but without Norma Berryhill's diligence as mentor, counselor and confidante to hundreds of students' and physicians' wives while their husbands spent long hours away from them in service to the hospital, it's hard to imagine the success the hospital has known. The doors of their spacious home on West Franklin Street (on the north side, just west of Church Street) opened to provide meals to many of the men serving with Norma's husband and any wife needing guidance. Their youngest daughter, Cat Berryhill Williams, said that when she and Jane would come home from school, if one of their upstairs bedroom doors was closed, they knew that their mother was in

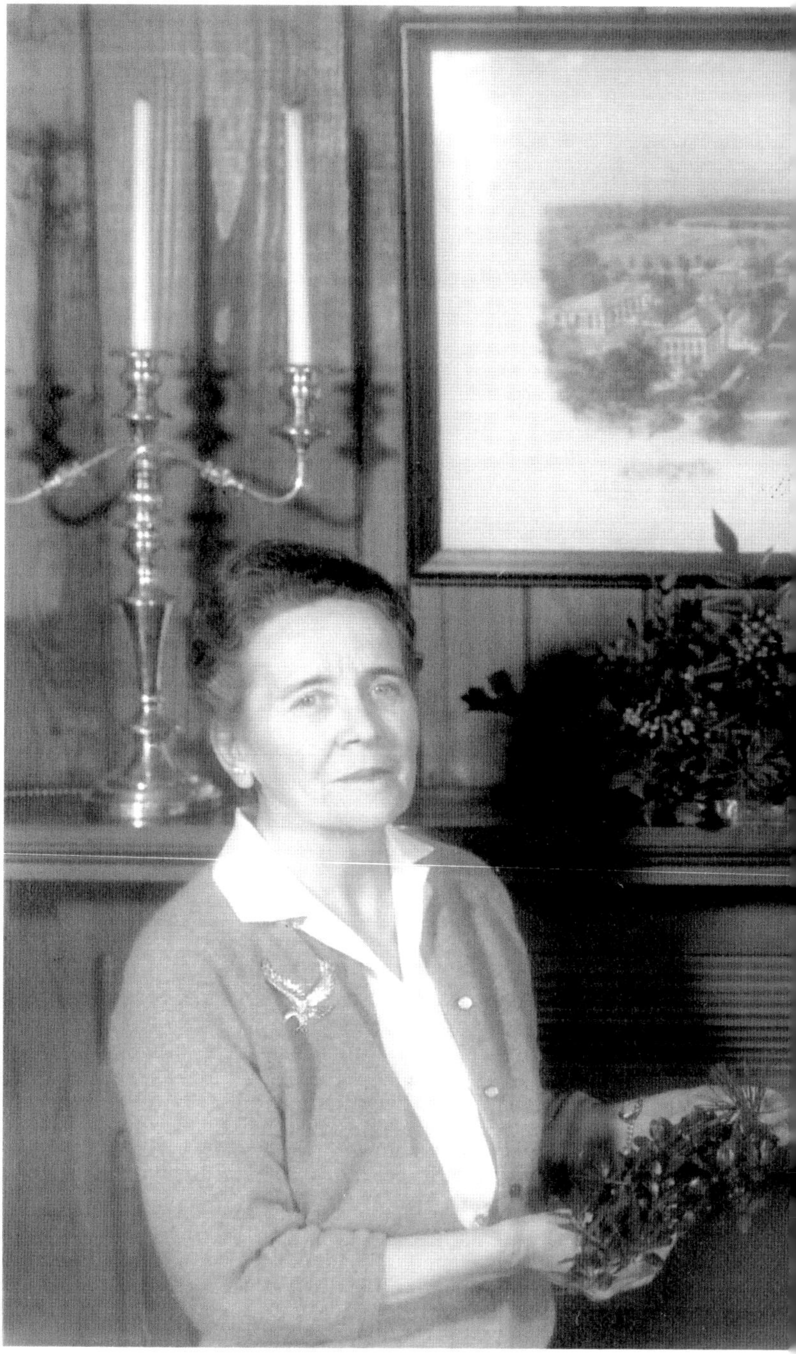

Norma Berryhill decorates the mantel at the family's home in the "country," circa 1960s; a rendering of the university campus hangs above. *Courtesy the Berryhill family.*

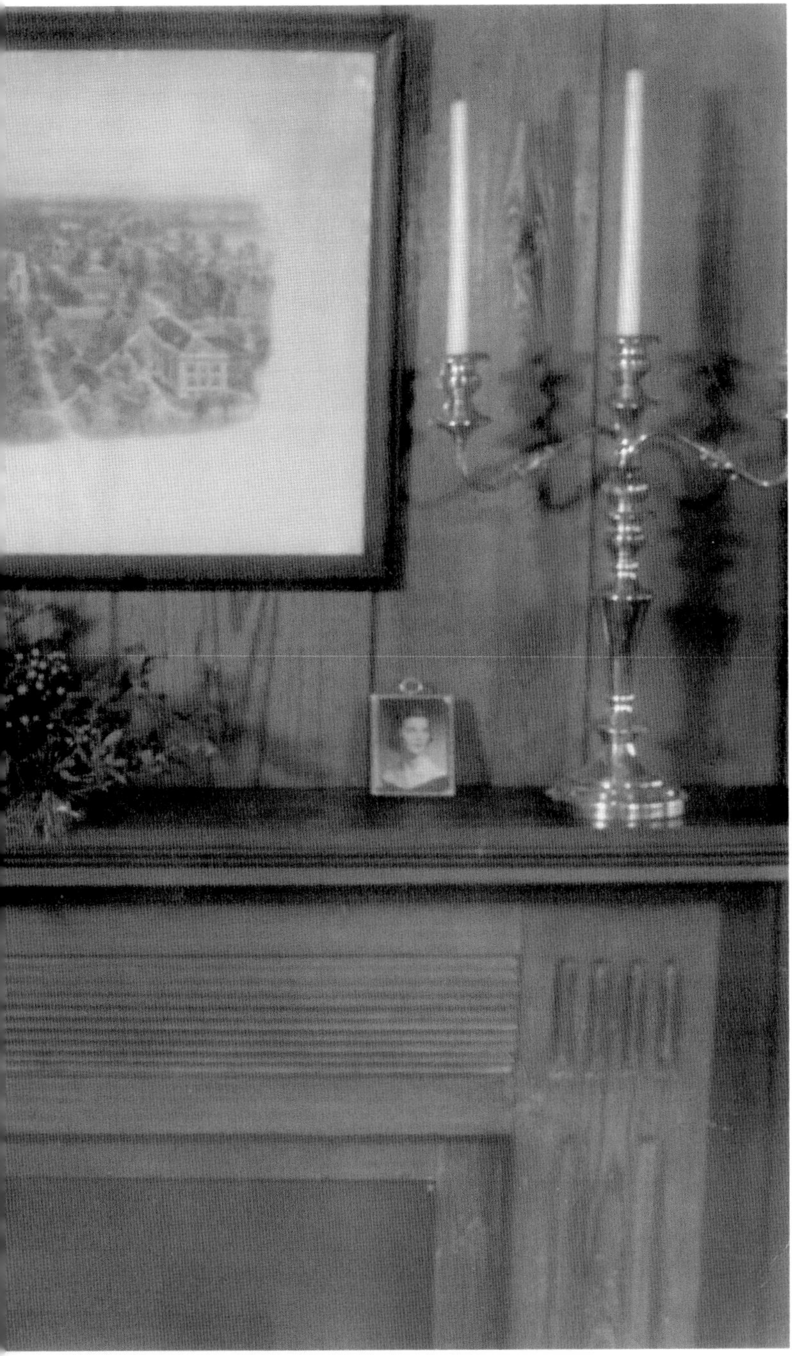

there counseling a distraught wife. She also noted the years of "waiting on the tables" and the continual stacks of dishes the two sisters washed throughout their childhood. "There was never a caterer," Williams said of the meals and parties that her mother provided for students and/or staff. The parties continued after the family moved to "the country," and Norma began to raise cattle. She sold the property in 1990, and it was developed as the Berryhill neighborhood of Carrboro.

Through the years, many awards and honors were bestowed, and in 1973, the Basic Medical Sciences Building on campus was renamed Berryhill Hall. Davidson College (where Dr. Berryhill had initially planned to matriculate) had given him an honorary doctor of science degree in 1956; UNC bestowed him with an honorary doctor of science in 1976; and he was designated as a master of the American College of Physicians in 1977. He died in 1979, but Norma lived to the age of 103, and up to her dying day (July 8, 2005) the women she provided empathy for not only remembered her but also visited her, showing appreciation for her support during times when they doubted their ability to hang on as wife of a doctor. Her contributions were recognized by the School of Medicine and UNC Hospitals with the Distinguished Service Award in 1975 and a lecture series named the Norma Berryhill Distinguished Lectureship, which takes place each fall, featuring an accomplished faculty member of the School of Medicine.

University of North Carolina Woman's Club

Among the many challenges faced by Norma Berryhill, one of the larger ones was helping her husband persuade physicians to make the move to a town with only one hotel and few restaurants. "Women from the North, West and Midwest thought of Chapel Hill as the country," Berryhill said. "If a housewife wanted a can of pineapple or sardines, she had to go all the way to Durham to get it. Chapel Hill was not sophisticated." Welcoming the wives of new medical faculty members fell to her, and she handled it brilliantly, assisting in finding housing or offering a casserole or dessert. Additionally, as the hospital was being built, she organized the Medical Student Wives Club and the House Officers Wives Club, both

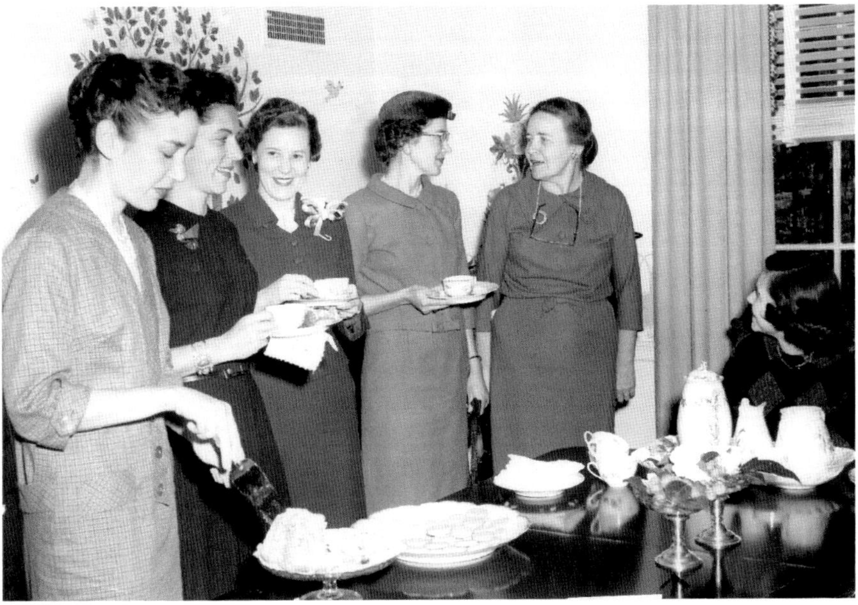

Norma Berryhill, with glasses around neck, hosts an early University Woman's Club meeting at the Carolina Inn, circa 1950s. *Courtesy the Berryhill family.*

of which built community among the women—helping them infuse their husbands, who were interns, residents and doctors.

Beyond the university's medical community, she helped found and, during the 1949–50 school year, serve as first president of the University Woman's Club, patterned after the club set up by the wives of the state legislators. "They were the Sir Walter Cabinet, and they were active while the legislators were in session," Berryhill said. "We thought that if we got them to visit, that would be a good idea," since the school was supported by state money. The UNC club invited the women of the Sir Walter Cabinet over for lunch once a year, giving them the opportunity to see the work being done at the school and the hospital. "We felt the more they knew about it, the more interested they would be," Berryhill said. She sat with other honored guests at the luncheon celebrating the fiftieth anniversary of the club in 2000.

Sally Vilas, daughter of the late Else Couch (who followed Berryhill as president of the club), honored her mother by wearing a pair of her gloves to the luncheon. "I never told anybody they had to wear a hat or gloves," Berryhill said. But pictures that Mary Pringle found in back issues of the *Chapel Hill News* show that they clearly did. While Pringle created a display depicting the history and evolution over the years, she learned that when new faculty would arrive in town the women of the club would call on the wife, leaving calling cards inside the door if she was not home. When she asked Berryhill about that, it was confirmed. "We had engraved cards we would leave," Berryhill said. "We welcomed new women into our community."

The University Woman's Club mission has been to "offer the community opportunities for friendship, social activities, intellectual stimulation, and service to the University." It is open to any woman associated with the university, either as faculty, staff, administration or the spouse of such—though in the early days the members were all wives. Activity groups (book discussions, bridge, antiques, etc.) and contributions to a scholarship fund have become part of membership.

President emeritus Bill Friday—the only man at the anniversary celebration—sat at the table with, among others, Berryhill and Gladys Coates (fourth president of the club). He was there as guest speaker and opened his remarks by addressing Berryhill and Coates, admitting that being in their presence was intimidating. "And I want you to know it," he said, before proceeding to entrance the 192 women in attendance. He said that during the previous week, following Berryhill's ninety-eighth birthday, he had called her and they had visited by phone, reminiscing about "Chapel Hill in the late forties, and those exciting days for returning veterans, a burgeoning community and a changing culture." Friday was assistant dean of men when the club began. He guided the group on a trip that for some was a tour down memory lane and, for others, painted a picture of the village that Chapel Hill had been. This trip included Doc Sutton at his drugstore, Sutton's Drugs (still in business since 1923), Papa Danziger at his Old World Coffee Shop, Mr. Foister at his camera and gift shop and Y.Z. Cannon at his barbershop. "The Bank of Chapel Hill and its great clock were in the middle of the street, and almost every summer morning, Mr. Eubanks, the bank president; Carl Durham, our congressman; John Umstead, our legislator; and Norman Cordon, the Metropolitan baritone who retired here, would visit," Friday said, continuing across East Franklin Street with more descriptions. "It was a way of life to remember. A way of life now gone forever."

Then, because he was addressing women who had daily been involved in the life of the university, he spoke of the changes there and the impact made on it by women. "Today, women are the dominant enrollment," Friday said. "Women have headed the law school, the College of Arts and Sciences and numerous departments and schools. Doris Betts became chairperson of the faculty. Indeed, the University campus system is headed by a woman [President Molly Broad] for the first time in its history!" He mentioned economic struggles in education in North Carolina, saying, "The university will be made stronger soon simply because the people will demand it. The people love and believe in Chapel Hill." Not surprisingly, Friday received a standing ovation and sat down, clearly moved. At the meeting's close, women flocked over to greet him, reminding Bill Friday how revered an elder statesman he remained.

PART THREE

LIFE AFTER WORLD WAR II

...Sometimes when the Springtime
comes,
And the sifting moonlight falls—
They'll think again of this night here
And these old brown walls,
Of white old well, and of old South
With bells deep booming tone,
They'll think again of Chapel Hill and—
Thinking—come back home...

–*Thomas Wolfe*

There was never a good war or a bad peace.

–*Benjamin Franklin*

From its first days until 1946, every day at the University of North Carolina included chapel. Into the twentieth century, chapel began at sunrise, with everyone enrolled required to attend. Generally lasting half an hour, it provided students the opportunity to learn from their university president, the primary speaker at these convocations. The chapel assemblies ended when the campus became inundated with students following World War II and schedules could no longer accommodate it.

The town had to make accommodations with the increase as well —quite literally. The 1940 census lists 3,654 as the population of Chapel Hill; by 1950 it had almost tripled, to 9,177. The town began to grow outside its limits, with students renting every available space—spare bedrooms, attics, basements, porches, barns and at least one chicken coop—that was within walking distance to campus. Besides new on-campus housing for couples, the first apartment community, called Glen Lennox, was built on the southeast side of town, down the big hill from the university on the road to Raleigh. Many professors and their families moved into the garden-style (rather than "stacked") complexes, which still provide a comfortable lifestyle for renters. Professors and a small enclave of nurses started moving to "the country" when, in 1952, the first suburb, Dogwood Acres, about three miles south of town off the road to Pittsboro, began to be developed from a forest that had been mostly cleared in 1949, except for the dogwood trees, which were soon accompanied by the recurring woodlands in any place not regularly mowed.

The ensuing building boom became a way of life as citizens learned to appreciate undeveloped land while it remained. The village grew into a town, though its inhabitants would long deny it, as the village spirit remained true.

A "SNAPSHOT" OF LIFE

An old photo can certainly get a story started. One day this photograph arrived in the mail from Nashville, sent by Ann Gobbel Sullivan, wife of Noel (front row, far right, in white pants). Intrigued, I called her and she said, "My mother-in-law, the late Bernadine Sullivan, a Chapel Hill High School English teacher for many years, had saved it. I thought it was the cutest picture." It was taken in 1945, sometime around V-Day from the look of the trees, the clothes of warm but not sweltering weather and the depth of hope and promise on the faces. The troops would soon be returning home, but these lads had been doing their part at home as members of the Safety Patrol at Chapel Hill Elementary School.

"We helped kids when they went across the street," said Stanley Peele (first on left, back row). The school was near the busiest intersection in

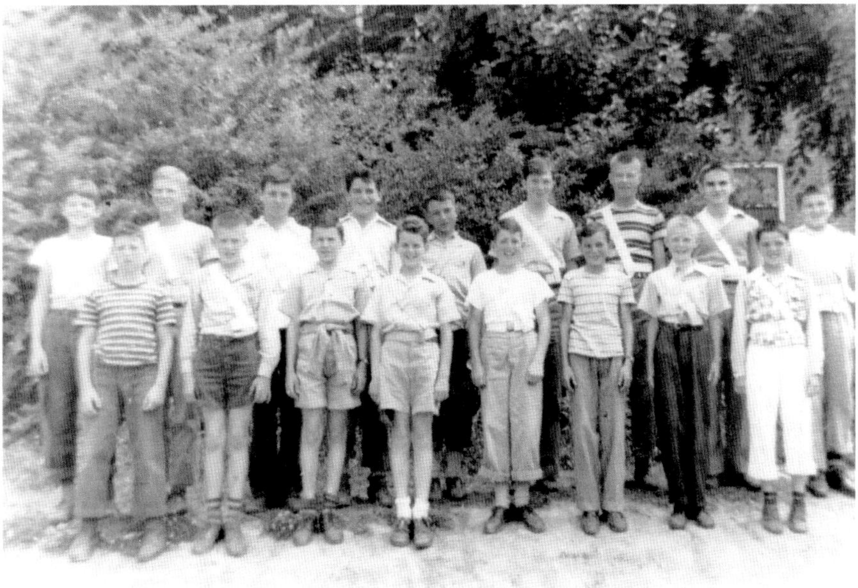

Members of the Safety Patrol. *Back row, left to right*: Stanley Peele, Fenno McGinty, unidentified, Tom Maultsby, Portis Welch, Davis Tournage, Jack Bright, Lewis Philips and Jack Maultsby. *Front row*: Alex Shepard, John Gwynn, R.B. Fitch, Pat Webb, John Earnhardt, Sydney Sparrow, Ronald Scherill and Noel Sullivan. *Courtesy the Gobbel family.*

town at the corner of Franklin and Columbia Streets where University Square is now, a few yards away from the only traffic light the town then had. John Earnhardt (fourth from right, front row) said they were standing on the playground, where much of their lunchtimes were spent playing volleyball. Peele, who went on to become a chief district court judge and still serves as an emergency judge, remembered his favorite way to spend lunch in those days. Across Franklin Street, where Kinko's is today, there was a Pure Oil gas station next door to Walker's Funeral Home, which has been there since 1924. Peele recalled that he would go to the "filling station" and buy his lunch for one dime. "I'd get one of those long, narrow bags of peanuts and a bottle of Pepsi," Peele said. "I'd take two sips—not one and not three, but two sips—and pour all the bag of peanuts in there and it would fizz up, and then I'd chug-a-lug it," he said, even relishing the memory of the subsequent belching. "It was a good meal."

Maybe that's why they all look so skinny. "I was so thin I couldn't keep my socks up," said R.B. Fitch (third from left, front row). He wasn't allowed to play volleyball or go to the filling station during lunch. "I went home for lunch every day. My parents kept me on a very short leash," he said, laughing. He would cross Franklin Street and walk past Walker's to his home behind the funeral home. His father owned Fitch's Lumber Company in Carrboro, and starting in 1974, R.B. and his wife, Jenny, developed a 640-acre piece of land in Chatham County that they named Fearrington Village, which by 2009 was home to over 1,800 residents and an award-winning country inn and restaurant. As to the no-nonsense expression on his face in the photo, Fitch said, "I was a very serious patrol officer—no smiles—don't mess with me," and he again erupted into laughter. He said that most of the boys were active with the Boy Scouts and volunteered to become Safety Patrol officers.

They were called into duty during football games at Kenan Stadium, as well. "We guarded the gates near the field of Kenan Stadium," Peele said. Fitch remembered the day when a fire broke out on Raleigh Road during a game. "Somebody came on the PA and announced, 'All Boy Scouts please assemble at the south end of the field to fight a forest fire.' We trotted down, and there was a brush fire we beat out, then came back and guarded the gates," Fitch said. "I was very proud of myself. I put myself in a hero class."

A few years younger than most of the boys in the photo, Ann Sullivan remembered those days well. "You could walk all over Chapel Hill. I rode my bike to school" from her home on University Drive. Her father, Temple "Tony" Gobbel, worked at the Bank of Chapel Hill, which was next to Eubanks Drug Store in the center of downtown East Franklin Street. She said that to get home, "He had to walk through the store, and he would sometimes come home with chocolate," a rare treat in those days. Sullivan also recalled that when she was in high school, her father almost took a job offer in Burlington, but she was so devastated by the news that her father, who served on the Chapel Hill School Board, in Kiwanis and with the Red Cross, declined the offer. Not only Sullivan but also the community benefited from that decision. Many newspaper clippings saved by her mother, Virginia, illustrate their level of commitment to Chapel Hill, summed up in a July 1968 *Durham Morning Herald* story released upon his retirement:

> *J.T. Gobbel's long and productive career with The Bank of Chapel Hill and, after the merger, with North Carolina National Bank has been paralleled by his long and productive role as a leader in this community.*
>
> *His influence has been felt in virtually every facet of community life here—in business, public schools, charitable organizations, church work, civic projects, public recreation, industry-hunting for the County. Wherever significant efforts were being made to do something for the community, Tony Gobbel could be counted among the leaders.*

"My parents stayed here all their lives, and my mother moved into Carolina Meadows soon after it opened," Sullivan said.

At the time of the picture in this section, the high school was located next to the elementary school, built at a time when clear-cutting prior to building was a futuristic concept. "It was a lovely school," Fitch said of the elementary school and the wooded grounds. "The high school wasn't much, but the elementary school had balance and a wonderful front yard." Earnhardt concurred, saying, "There was a wooded area near the school," across from where Panera Bread now sits.

As to the rolled-up pants that Earnhardt, Sullivan and some of the others wore, Earnhardt said it was the style.

Leaving one's hometown would apparently become the style as well, as many of the seventeen boys in the photograph left the area after graduation. Alex Shepard became a pilot for Delta Airlines, Sydney Sparrow moved to Boston, Lewis Phillips moved to South America, Davis Tournage moved to the Burlington area, Jack Bright moved to Colorado and, of course, Noel Sullivan moved to Nashville. Fenno McGinty was deceased, as was Jack Maultsby, who built and ran the Farm House restaurant with his wife, Chapel Hill native Anne Umstead. "I tried to box with Jack one time—but never again," Peele remembered. "Jack was an all-knowing person about mechanical stuff and driving an automobile. He drove a vehicle long before he had a license. Tom Maultsby was a gentleman beyond gentlemen." Peele also remembered coveting something that Sid Sparrow often had. "He was a really decent sort, an intelligent man. He came to school with something I had a yearning for—cheese crackers." It was nothing more than slices of cheddar on saltines, but Peele said he'd swap his peanuts and Pepsi for the cheese crackers when he could get Sparrow to agree.

"It was a different time around Chapel Hill," Earnhardt said. "There weren't so many people around here then." There were so few people there was only one class per grade. But soon, the most sudden population increase of the century would occur as returning veterans moved to Chapel Hill bent on using the free education afforded by the GI Bill.

Bill and Ida Friday

In 1946, with droves of newly attached couples invading Chapel Hill, it's doubtful that William Clyde Friday, a native of Dallas in Gaston County, and Ida Howell Friday, of Lumberton six counties away in Robeson County, stood out in the village in which an institute would one day be named after them. They had married on May 13, 1942, after meeting on a blind date while both studied in Raleigh—Bill at North Carolina State University and Ida at Meredith College. Bill, though dismayed when his parents separated after he started college (spending his first year at Wake Forest), had become president of his class and was the first student of a state school to speak at commencement exercises when he graduated with a degree in textile engineering in 1941.

Though they'd been married four years on arrival in Chapel Hill, Bill had served in the U.S. Navy during World War II, stationed at the Naval Ammunitions Depot in Norfolk, Virginia. He might have been spared the front lines, but with an engineering degree, his promotion to plant operations manager put him in a tense situation twenty-four hours a day with some five hundred tons of explosives situated ten yards from his barracks. He later commented that after arriving at UNC only seven days after discharge, it took a long while before he was conditioned not to jump whenever someone lit a match, which plenty of people frequently did in those days.

Pulling into Chapel Hill in a two-door Chevrolet, Ida's mission was a master's degree in public health, while Bill was there for a law degree. Their first pursuit, however, was for a place to hang their hats. "We looked for a place to live, which was difficult to find," Bill said. "But we were

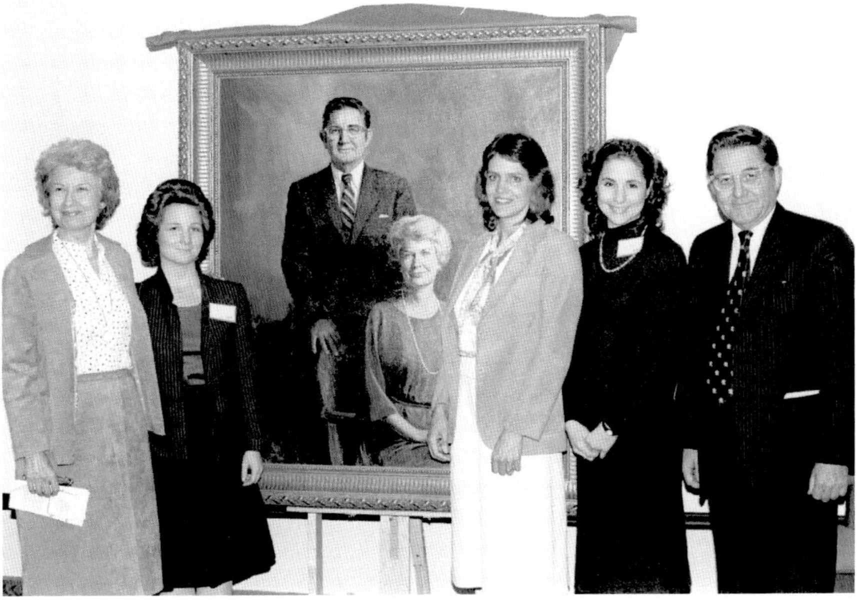

William and Ida Friday in front of the portrait painted of them upon his retirement as president of the University of North Carolina system; they are joined by daughters Fran, Mary and Betsy. *Courtesy North Carolina Collection, University of North Carolina Library at Chapel Hill.*

determined. We walked down Cameron Street." Ida continued, "We got near a house and saw a person outside who lived there and, Bill said, 'I know that man.' We knocked on his door and his wife said, 'Come on in—I'll give you a place to stay.'" They were grateful for the attic room, where a peg in the wall served to hang their few garments. But sanctuary would be short-lived.

Ida said, "The next day came, and she said she had company coming—'You've got to go.' She took the clothes off the wall and put them out by the car." Ida stood waiting at the car as Bill dragged himself back from classes. "It was my first day in law school," Bill said. "It was a dreary day, and I had seven cases, all in Latin, that I had to somehow translate, and I looked across and there she is with all our worldly possessions." Welcome back to civilian life, Lieutenant Friday!

They found shelter that day down the hill on South Columbia Street in a one-room house across the street from Ebb and Merritt's filling station, now Merritt's Store (famous for the best BLTs in the Triangle). After receiving her degree, Ida started a post that she held from 1948 to 1952 with the School of Public Health as an instructor (among the first women to teach there) and workshop director. Here she met Lucy Morgan, who became her mentor as they assisted faculty members at North Carolina Central University, which was then known as the North Carolina School for Negroes. The two women, working together, in what at the time was not recognized as groundbreaking work, established programs that continue today at the school in Durham. Because of Ida's work, when Bill graduated from law school in 1948, they remained in Chapel Hill and he was soon working in the office of the dean of students, Fred H. Weaver—Bill's first job in an administration career that he had never envisioned and that would include serving as president of the University of North Carolina for thirty years, beginning in 1956.

As their family grew with three daughters, Fran, Mary and Betsy, Ida stopped working outside of the home and concentrated on the career that pushed them all forward, as mother, great supporter of her husband and the university and as an active volunteer using her resources to improve Chapel Hill. She helped found many of the organizations in which she served—the Chapel Hill Preservation Society, the Community Church, the ArtsCenter of Carrboro, the Women's Center, the Triangle Community Foundation and the American Dance Festival, among others. She received numerous awards: the North Carolina Distinguished Service Award for Women, the North Carolina Public Service Award (awarded jointly with Bill), the President's Award of the UNC School of Public Health Alumni Association and the Cornelia Phillips Spencer Bell Award.

The Bell Award ceremony was held in April 2003 on the 178th anniversary of the birth of Cornelia Phillips Spencer, best known as the woman who, besides naming the Davie Poplar, climbed to the top of South Building on March 20, 1875, following Reconstruction, and rang the university's bell, announcing the good news that the school would reopen. Spencer had endeavored through her writings during the Civil War to keep people of the state informed as students left to join the battle, but classes continued even with enrollment down from 456 students prewar to 50 in 1865 and after great damage was done to the campus while troops camped there as the final terms ending the war were ironed out in Durham. This damage, and corresponding events as documented by Spencer and others, forced the school to close after the war's end. Since 1994, UNC's bicentennial year, the Bell Award has been given to a woman known for her outstanding contributions to the university, while noting Spencer's voice.

The George Watts Hill Alumni Center was the place to be that Thursday afternoon, but the word on everyone's lips was "Ida," as she was recognized for her years of dedication to the learning institution, the town and the state of North Carolina. "She was an extremely popular choice," said Anne Dellinger, one of the eight selection committee members and a professor in the UNC School of Government. "I had known her as the university president's wife…and her contributions to the university and community. What I did not know was what she did as a young woman." She had not known that Ida Friday had blazed the trail for women as one of the first to teach at the University of North Carolina at Chapel Hill. "She must have been something," Dellinger said admiringly.

Diane Kjervik, chair of the selection committee and director of the Carolina Women's Center, welcomed the hundred or so admirers in attendance, saying, "This is our opportunity to ring the bell for Ida Friday, Carolina's first lady," as she introduced then chancellor James Moeser, who presented the award.

"Ida Friday is the best-known name in Chapel Hill—with the possible exception of Bill Friday. Often, the two names are called as one—Bill and Ida Friday. Or simply, Bill-and-Ida," Moeser began.

> *Yet this one remarkable partnership is made up of two clearly equal partners and two very strong people. Both Ida and Bill Friday stand for social justice. They are attuned to the lives of people who struggle with life's inequities as a result of poverty, lack of education, race or gender. The Fridays have worked personally and professionally in their several spheres of influence to remove obstacles and provide opportunities for all.*

As she accepted her award, Ida Friday seemed most impressed by those who had come out to honor her. "I look over this audience," she said, and her eyes fell upon Zora Rashkis. "I see the wonderful schoolteacher who called me about our daughter Mary…" But before she could continue, Mary, who had come with her husband, John Leadbetter, from London, interrupted her. "That was Fran—" Mary Friday Leadbetter called out, eliciting laughter from the audience. Regardless, Ida knew that Rashkis had turned a daughter around that year. Ida also knew her accomplishments here had much to do with the place and the people in it. "Thank you for making our lives so rich and full for fifty-seven years," she said. "What else can I say?" Nothing else was needed for the people to stand and applaud.

Part of the Carolina Women's Center's mission is the celebration of women as shapers of the world, Kjervik said after the ceremony. "Ida Friday is a beautiful example of a woman who has shaped Chapel Hill, North Carolina and the country in terms of a positive role model, as a partner with her husband and as a woman with her own public policy agenda," she said.

In attendance at the ceremony was Miranda Mullen, the daughter of Fran Friday and her husband, Jack Mullen. "I've grown up around her," Mullen said of Ida, her grandmother, who is also a painter and sculptor and whom she credited with leading her to study art history at UNC, where she was then a junior. "Whenever I'd go visit, she'd pick up artifacts [collected from travels] and go into stories about how they were made," Mullen said. She had traveled with her grandparents to Paris, where they celebrated their fiftieth wedding anniversary.

"Can you imagine anyone more deserving than Ida Friday?" asked Molly Broad, then president of the UNC system and resident of the house on East Franklin Street where the Fridays had lived for thirty years. "She is an institution and is beloved by everyone who has known her here for over fifty years—and those of us here even less time," Broad said.

"Ida is to Bill what Eleanor Roosevelt was to FDR," said Joel Schwartz, an adjunct in the department of public policy. He remembered a handwritten note received from Bill Friday when he had joined the faculty in 1968. "I never knew somebody so caring about people—he's a man for all seasons. And Ida's been his inextricable partner in his continuing process of caring." Then he paraphrased Winston Churchill, saying, "Never have two people done so much for all the citizens of North Carolina."

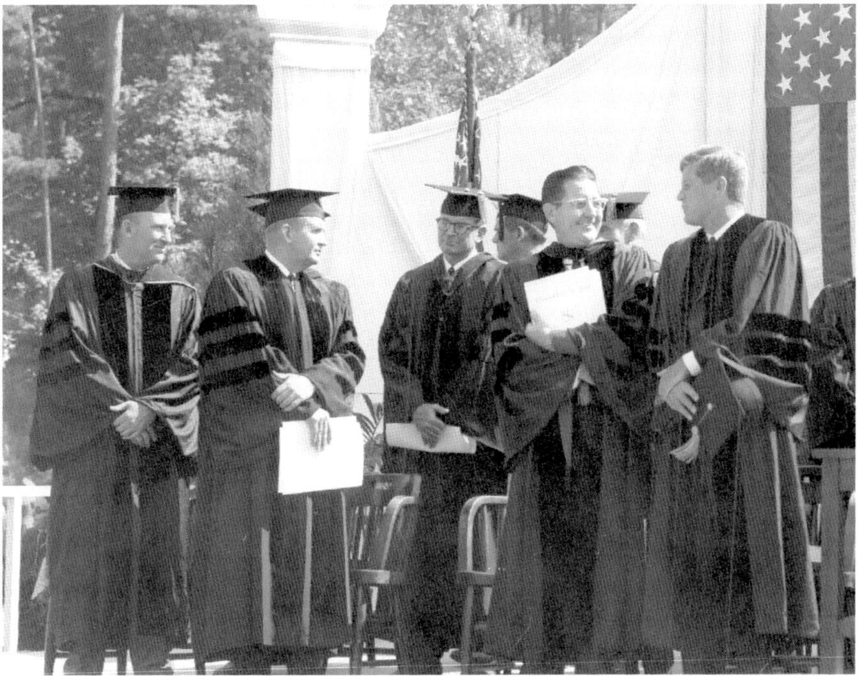

On October 12, 1961, University Day had even more pomp as President John F. Kennedy joined the celebration at Kenan Stadium. North Carolina governor Terry Sanford is standing on the right among others. *Courtesy North Carolina Collection, University of North Carolina Library at Chapel Hill.*

"She has invested her heart and soul in the University of North Carolina and in the people who live here," Moeser said, and he concluded with, "She has endeavored to make this university community a much better place for *all* its citizens."

There were hard times for the family along the way—the civil rights movement, the speaker ban law, the Vietnam War protests and a night in the early 1970s when the Fridays huddled in the middle of the president's mansion with their daughters while students pelted the house with rocks for an hour. "The students weren't mad at us," Bill Friday said.

> *They had tensions that needed to be released. That's a great part about being in Chapel Hill, and I said that to President Nixon the day after Kent State* [the May 4, 1970 war protest at Kent State University in Ohio turned into a bloodbath when the Ohio National Guard

> killed four students and injured nine]. *But he didn't understand then, and I don't think he ever did understand. We had five thousand students protesting between South Building and Wilson Library. Not a single shot was fired and not a single class failed to be taught. They started here to understand that to be free they must be responsible.*

In 1984, the Fridays were recipients of the North Caroliniana Society award and were honored in 1988 when the name chosen for a new off-campus site was the William and Ida Friday Continuing Education Center, which opened in 1991. In 2004, they were further honored when Governor Mike Easley and the North Carolina legislature bestowed on them the Long Leaf Pine Award for lifelong service to the state.

In 1986, at age sixty-five, Friday retired as president emeritus, yet even at age eighty-eight, he continued another job held for over three decades with UNC-TV, hosting its longest-running program, *North Carolina People*. He recognized long ago that it is the people of North Carolina who make it special. "We've never had a wealthy state…but what's so wonderful here is we have an atmosphere of open and free discussion," Friday said. "We are so blessed with all of our state's natural endowments…but most of all it's the spirit of our people. It's important to know what's happening and to be a part of that. I want to make a difference because that's what we're here for." He has certainly achieved that. The many things he did that made a difference during his tenure at UNC included helping form the Atlantic Coast Conference (the ACC, in which the UNC Tar Heels have realized many championships in an array of sports); sponsoring North Carolina public television; and developing Research Triangle Park, which has offered a field of career choices for young people graduating from the local universities so the state can retain its young talent. It was under Friday's leadership that the sixteen-campus Consolidated System was transformed into the UNC System in 1972. But during all that he did for the school, Friday and his family were approachable members of the Chapel Hill community. To this day, their almost weekly arrival at the Carrboro Farmers Market on Saturday mornings generally sends a ripple through the Carrboro Commons as people naturally congregate around their "first couple" with greetings.

Kay and Georgia Kyser

A lasting friendship started during the early 1950s soon after another couple arrived in town. Kay and Georgia Kyser dramatically changed their lives in 1951 when they moved from Beverly Hills, California, via New York City into the historic home of Kay's uncle, Vernon Howell. Howell had been a professor of chemistry and was founder of the School of Pharmacy, for which he served as dean from 1901 until his death in 1931, and for whom Howell Hall was named. As UNC chancellor emeritus Robert B. House described in his book, *The Light That Shines*:

> *Vernon Howell was in himself a uniquely individual personality in this community noted for its characters. Shy almost to the point of introversion, he nevertheless dominated our imaginations by his fearless genuineness and courage to be himself. His impact on the undergraduate mind was dramatic…Nothing human is more engaging than a disciplined and well-stocked mind. Students are thrilled by it. And we rejoiced that in Vernon Howell we had one.*

Around the turn of the nineteenth century, Professor Howell had bought the house at 504 East Franklin Street, which had been built in 1814 by William Hooper, grandson and namesake of a signer of the Declaration of Independence. Several generations of Hoopers later, Professor Manuel Fetter, who taught Greek at UNC, bought the house and raised three daughters and four sons there. Other professors later owned it, including H.V.P. Wilson, UNC's first professor of biology. House continued in his book, saying:

> [Howell] *was a bachelor and rejoiced in the historic significance of his old house on Franklin Street…one of the ancient landmarks of Chapel Hill. Dean Howell lived as he pleased in the old house. He did not care to fix it up. He kept his car, "Old Wheeze," parked on the front walk…His home was always open to his students…Also at his house his professional colleagues from all over North Carolina loved to gather…Vernon Howell was an inspiration to all around him in science, humanity, and culture.*

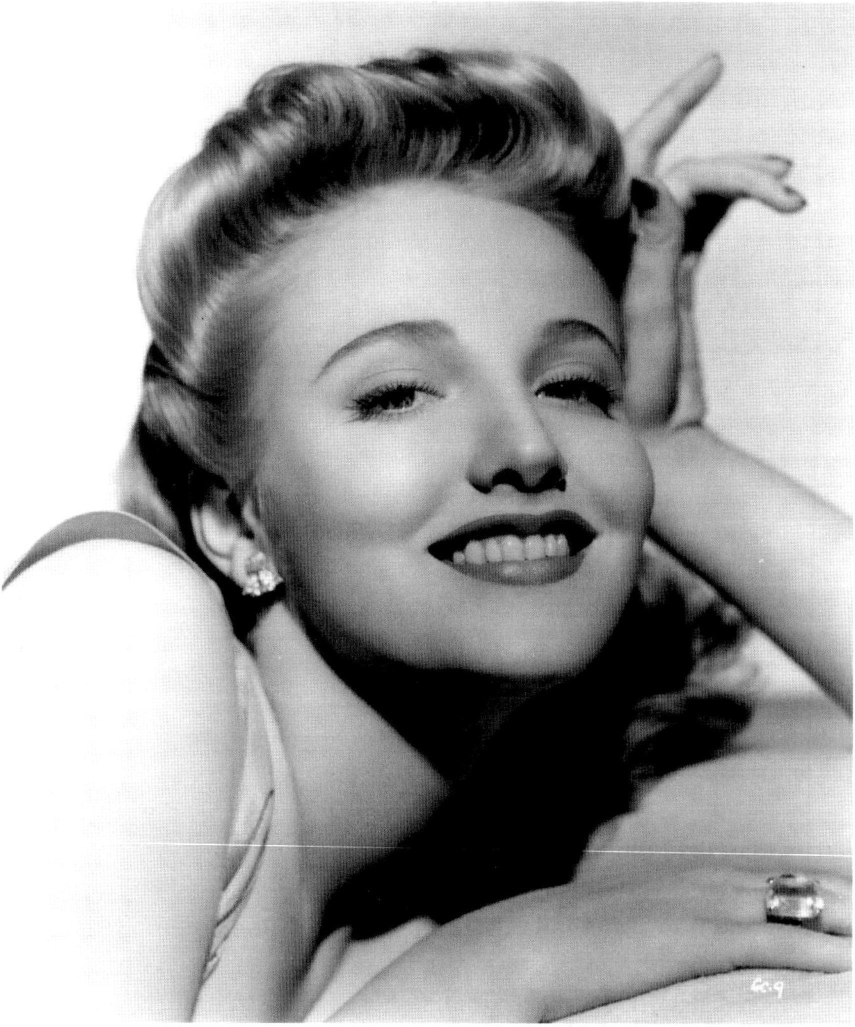

The glamour days of Georgia Carroll before she married bandleader Kay Kyser. *Courtesy Georgia Kyser.*

Their father was a pharmacist, but Vernon trained his sister, Emily Royster Howell Kyser—a famous talker who never cooked—who became the first female registered pharmacist in North Carolina; and he made himself available to her three sons.

After a childhood that included many days playing under the magnolias and oaks of his Uncle Vernon's Federal-style farmhouse with single chimneys on both ends, James Kern "Kay" Kyser, a native of Rocky Mount, probably never thought of attending any school other than UNC–Chapel Hill. Far from his mind, however, would have been the career he gained as a result of his time there. While a student, he became a cheerleader and fast friends with Hal Kemp, the leader of the UNC band, who diverted Kay from the career path chosen by his parents and other relatives who had become pharmacists. Kemp sought fame and fortune in New York and handed the baton to Kyser, who dropped the James of his name, adapting his middle initial into the alliterative name that launched a lucrative career after he graduated a year later and took the band on the road. "Kay didn't want to become a pharmacist or a bandleader," said his widow, Georgia Carroll Kyser. "He couldn't play an instrument; he didn't read music or know anything about music, but he was a good organizer of men and fun to be around, and his friend talked him into taking his place." Not that Georgia was anywhere in the picture at that point—she had been but three years old and living in her native Dallas, Texas, when Kyser entered UNC.

Georgia's career blossomed while she was little more than a bud herself. Her Aunt Edna took an early interest in Georgia, paying to have her teeth straightened, teaching her about fashion on shopping trips to Neiman Marcus and, upon graduation from high school, escorting her niece on a cruise from the Gulf of Mexico to New York City. Not many Texans arrive in the Big Apple aboard a cruise boat, but when Georgia Carroll disembarked, a career was launched. "The Rise of Georgia" was the title of a picture page in *Redbook* magazine, showing the stunning blue-eyed blonde, "5-foot 9-inches in stockinged feet." She was seventeen, but instead of matriculating at the University of Texas, she stayed in New York. "They were looking for someone like me," Kyser said. Today she would be called a supermodel. By 1941, she was under contract to Warner Brothers and, with the money she had saved from modeling, bought a small house in Hollywood's Coldwater Canyon, where she moved with her mother, who kept her grounded.

In the meantime, Kay Kyser—"the Ol' Professor of *Swing*" as he was known—continued with great success. "He made the highest salary of anybody with a big band," Georgia said. He commanded a top-ten radio program for ten years (Kollege of Musical Knowledge) and starred in eight movies. "Both of us had success at the same time," and then the war brought them together while turning their talents to USO shows shortly after Pearl Harbor. Georgia quickly recognized the intelligence and decorum involved with Kay Kyser and his band members, with whom she was soon singing. "He was very particular with who he took on—they were college-educated, there was no rough language…his bus had a fun, upbeat atmosphere," Georgia said.

They married in 1944 and Kay moved into Georgia's charming cottage, where Kimberly and Carol were born. Two moves later, including a brief stint in New York, the death of Kyser's mother in 1950 and dissatisfaction with the show business lifestyle, turned Kay's focus toward North Carolina and the house left vacant in 1931 by Uncle Vernon's death. "He wanted out of showbiz. He wanted to live simply. He wanted to live the way he wanted to live," Georgia said. "The Kyser family thought that Chapel Hill was the center of the universe. 'Wait until you go to Chapel Hill,' they said, 'it's the quaintest, most wonderful place you can imagine.'" When they arrived and drove down Franklin Street on the way to the Carolina Inn, Georgia must have blinked. "I said, 'Where is this quaint village?'"

She would soon learn, but not before all thoughts of simply moving into Uncle Vernon's house were dashed on first look at the kudzu-, honeysuckle- and wisteria vine–covered two-story house with side-gabled roof. It needed more than the taming of nature around it. "We had to re-plaster, re-plumb and rewire it," she said. "There was so much wisteria covering it, it required a bulldozer. It was too run-down to live in." So while work began on the house, they made Rocky Mount their home base with their daughters. They would later add a wing onto the house that included a new kitchen and family room; and a third daughter, Amanda, was born in 1952.

Georgia was not yet thirty when she moved to Chapel Hill, but it didn't take long for her to appreciate the old bakery, University Florist and Sutton's along with all else that the town had to offer. "We had our complete world," she said. "We didn't need anything except for that block—except for Fowler's." Fowler's was the food store, located on West Franklin Street—"the center for meeting friends," Georgia said.

Soon after moving into the house, they began to receive visitors. Georgia said that women would come to visit around 5:00 p.m., "when my daughters were wildly animated. I started collecting calling cards." When she asked what she was supposed to do with the cards, she was told that the custom was to "return the call." "I couldn't with three children," she said. So she and Kay changed the custom. "We threw a party at the Monogram Club—all ages came, and we had entertainment by an unknown young man who hung around the Playmakers for a long time after graduation—Andy Griffith."

Recovering a chance to further her education, Georgia began auditing classes at UNC until she struck on a course that required her to register and become a full-fledged student—a sculpture class—where the first friend she made was one for life: Ida Friday, who had a master's degree but had missed out on classes in the arts. Georgia continued her studies until nineteen years later, when she received a degree.

At the time that Georgia and Ida met, the Fridays lived nearby in a furnished house but had saved up money to buy their own home. When Bill Friday was named president of the North Carolina university system, they and their three daughters instead moved two houses down from the Kyser clan—and Georgia helped Ida buy furniture for the president's house. The two men hit it off, as well. Kay was continually visited by his Hollywood cronies (who would sneak into town, Bill Friday said) like Guy Lombardo or Bob Hope or Bill Stern, a famous sportscaster from the 1930s to the 1960s. "Kay called me one night when Ida and Georgia were out and told me to come over," Bill Friday said. "I walked over and saw two shadows in the driveway and one of them was Bill Stern. What a wonderful panoply, was the generosity of his heart. The four of us had a happy friendship for many years."

"Our house became the center for girl fun," Georgia said. By 1960, a pool large enough for racing had been built in the backyard. "It was bliss," said Kimberly Kyser. "It was like we had our own kingdom." The third floor of the house held the sunny playroom with dress-up clothes straight from Georgia's Hollywood and modeling days. "People loved to come play with us. My father came to this house all through his childhood to visit his uncle, and he played in the same boxwoods that we played in during the '50s and '60s," which a third generation of Kyser children has played in as well. "We played house in them they were so big, and they're still there," Kimberly said. They attended school at Chapel Hill Elementary School, where University Square is today. "We were required to walk to school everyday," Kimberly said. "My parents made us walk to school. There was no sense of anyone being in danger." Perhaps it was the pharmacy roots in their blood or the fact that they walked with the children of Mr. Sloan that led them to stop at Sloan's Drug Store (where Spanky's is now) on the way back from school, or at Sutton's Drugs. "The store owners looked after the children."

Georgia and Ida became instrumental in several endeavors still in existence, including founding the Preservation Society of Chapel Hill. With Georgia's interest in decorating, and her worldly knowledge, she recognized the charm of Chapel Hill and how easily it would be lost if the wrecking ball was not arrested. She had the ideas, but Ida had the courage and training to speak out with them, and thus they worked together, preserving many town treasures that would otherwise no longer exist. The Kysers exposed Ida to foreign travel, taking her with them for her first trip to Europe, which led to her continued travels until visiting every continent but Antarctica.

A true blue Tar Heel, Kay used his radio connections to assist Billy Carmichael and Bill Friday in bringing public television to UNC by helping secure a channel under authorization of the federal government. Having the channel helped to transform the UNC Department of Radio, established in 1947 with Earl Wynn as chairman, into the Department of Radio, Television and Motion Pictures, with Wynn as chair and director of the Communication Center. Kay Kyser also wrangled free equipment from NBC and recruited talent to help launch the first shows telecast on January 8, 1955, providing WUNC-TV with professional-quality broadcasts that have helped keep it broadcasting ever since.

As sophisticated as their past careers may have made them, the Kysers appreciated the eccentricity of Chapel Hill. Georgia said that Kay used to send his copy of the *Chapel Hill Weekly* to actor Walter Pigeon each week. "He would say there's just no newspaper with headlines like 'Rare bird sighted downtown,'" Georgia said of Pigeon.

Before Georgia met him, Kay had begun to suffer with pain in his feet. He tried everything available, and in the late 1940s, after medicine failed to relieve the arthritic condition that sometimes kept him in a wheelchair, he became a devotee of Christian Science philosophy. Of course it ran contrary to his family's medical legacy, but his devotion, not only to the healing but also to the depth of thought, led him to lecture, become a CS practitioner and run the film and television department of the church in Boston during the 1970s. His service begat him the honorary title of "President of the Worldwide Church of CS" in 1983.

Kay died of heart failure on July 23, 1985, at age eighty, leaving Bill Friday as male chaperone of the Georgia and Ida duo when they attended town and university functions and then to be the comforter and comforted when tragedy struck each family in the loss of a daughter—Carroll at age forty-five and Betsy at forty-four.

Chapel Hill High School Reunion

Midway through the twentieth century, some of the lads from the Safety Patrol found themselves graduating from high school. In the spring of 1950, seventy-two eager young Chapel Hillians were poised to begin the rest of their lives. For some, that meant going around the corner from the high school near the main intersection in town and onto the campus of the University of North Carolina. Others went away to college; some went into the family business, including farming, or to careers elsewhere. In April 2000, thirty-two of them gathered for a weekend of parties and fellowship. It all started on a Thursday evening with drinks and hors d'oeuvres at the Farmhouse Restaurant; Friday night's dinner banquet at the Carolina Inn; and a Saturday afternoon pig pickin' at John and Jean Earnhardt's home.

"At the reunions, you find out most have been pretty successful," John Earnhardt said. "They've had careers they've enjoyed and are active in churches and civic clubs—they're complete people." They had enjoyed a variety of careers—architecture, engineering, banking, teaching, working with Social Security, in medicine, in commercial real estate, as restaurateurs, farmers and more.

The high school building of those days had not been so complete. It had been built rather hurriedly after the previous building burned down.

"There was no auditorium, just one long classroom building and a house used for an office and overflow classroom," Ann Umstead Maultsby said. She was the daughter of the late John Wesley Umstead, founder of Umstead Hospital and an Orange County legislator and U.S. senator. "It was less than adequate facilities, but we were survivors." Something else that survived for Maultsby was her relationship with high school sweetheart Jack Maultsby. In June 2000, they celebrated forty-seven years of marriage. In 1950, Ann had been voted best girl athlete and Jack, most popular boy. They owned the Farmhouse Restaurant, and Jack was then president of the Central Carolina Vintage Car Club. Ann's interest in athletics had not diminished, but she had become a bench-sitter and avid fan of the Tar Heels, the women's basketball team.

Eddie Mann had been voted best all-around, and he lived up to the promise, enjoying a thirty-three-year career in banking, including becoming president of Orange Savings & Loan. He served on the Orange Water and Sewer Association (OWASA) board for eight years, shortly after the university got out of the utility business and the nonprofit agency was formed. He was chairman of the board during the tumultuous years when OWASA worked to establish the Cane Creek Reservoir. It was an especially difficult time for Mann because the strongest opposition to the project came from the Stanford family, the largest landowners in the area in which the reservoir would be created. "My wife is a Stanford," Mann said. They sat on opposite sides of the table but all ended well. "We remained married, and we're good friends." And Chapel Hill and Carrboro got a desperately needed water resource.

Raymond "Roscoe" Stainback arrived for the reunion from Atlanta, where he recently retired from an exciting career as an architect. His firm designed and built such projects as the Georgia Dome, where the 2000 Super Bowl was held, and the Omni and World Congress Center in Atlanta. "We miss Chapel Hill," Stainback said, speaking for himself and his wife, Catherine, whom he met at UNC. They moved to Atlanta in the 1960s during its boom years. "It's good to be there, but I'm always nostalgic for Chapel Hill."

Bobby Collins of Durham didn't crash the party, but neither did he graduate with the class. Only his sophomore year was spent at Chapel Hill High, but he formed friendships, which continued through the years as he enjoyed many of the class reunions. "I attended several high schools, and Chapel Hill High was the most accepting," Collins said. "It was the only one without cliques. They accepted people on face value."

Charles Creel came the greatest distance for the reunion—from Las Vegas, where he spent his career in real estate acquisitions for Howard Hughes. He bought some four hundred pieces of property and then, after Hughes's death, spent years contacting his heirs. Creel said that in twenty years of working for Hughes he never saw the man. "I dealt with him by memo…He didn't work with anyone directly except for his five aides."

Jesse Bell Lewis, the English and journalism teacher, attended the banquet, regaling her former students with funny stories about themselves. Their coach, Bill Grice, attended the pig pickin', and Mann remembered how hard they had struggled for uniforms when he played as a Tiger. "We had to furnish our own shoes, padding, uniform and equipment," he said.

"The [reunions] put things in perspective," Ann Maultsby said. "We really put on a push to get people to attend this year," she said. It paid off. "We've already gotten so many thank-you letters from people thanking us for making them come." For John Earnhardt, it felt like old times. "I don't think age is something you think that much about at these reunions," he said. "You're happy to still be able to do things. You enjoy hearing about people and their families."

More than half the class of 1950 still lived in the area. In addition to the ones mentioned above, the following were still part of the community: Tommy Bradshaw, Ann Farrell Cheek, Tommy Gravitt, Josie Hardee Thomas, William Hogan, Joseph Jones, June Lanning Caraway, Peggy Martindale Williams, Delbert Mayse, Donald Mullis, Jean Partin O'Daniel, Stanley Peele, Jo Rigsbee Cook, Julia Shields Evans, Catherine Smith Patterson, Waylan Stinson, Eleanor Thompson Ragan, Emogene Thompson Cole, Matt Thompson, Elinor Wagner Basnight and Betty Williams Layton.

PART FOUR

Struggles to Improve Life

When Chapel Hill was a village it was unmoneyed and egalitarian. What made people love it so? Partly the beauty of the place, partly the University atmosphere, where you could find friends in any field of endeavor, but above all it was the freedom in which we all lived.

—Cornelia Spencer Love

As hard as anybody would try to help or understand, in going through these experiences, these changes, I was by myself.

—Charlie Scott, UNC's first black basketball player, on changes for blacks in the 1960s

Chapel Hill has always been a predominantly white town, making up 76 percent of the population in the 1970s, which further illuminates the African American contributions to the campus and town, though they would not be recognized with a lasting commemoration on campus until the twenty-first century.

Archibald Henderson noted in *The Campus of the First State University* that in 1838 Professor Elisha Mitchell struck on a legendary marriage between utility and beauty by using the plethora of rocks extracted (or hit with each attempted dig with a shovel) to construct a rock wall around the perimeter of the campus. This eliminated piles of rock while providing an aesthetically pleasing and presumably low-maintenance way to keep wandering farm animals off-campus. "With slave labor to draw upon, the expense was inconsiderable as compared with the cost of such a project today" (written in 1949). It took six years to build that wall, using the stacking method rather than any adhesive material (by which time, the campus had doubtless grown beyond its boundaries, as it has never stopped growing), but maintenance on the rock walls may continue indefinitely. They last longer than wooden fences, but the ravages of nature (and sometimes cars) break them down eventually. Meanwhile, the men who have performed those duties for generations note with pride the walls they have worked on (which now include a cement core).

As previously learned, the university laundry provided clean and pressed clothing and linens to the student population via the tired and underpaid efforts of the black population, who also served as cooks, housekeepers, nursemaids, garden tenders, yard maintenance and in any

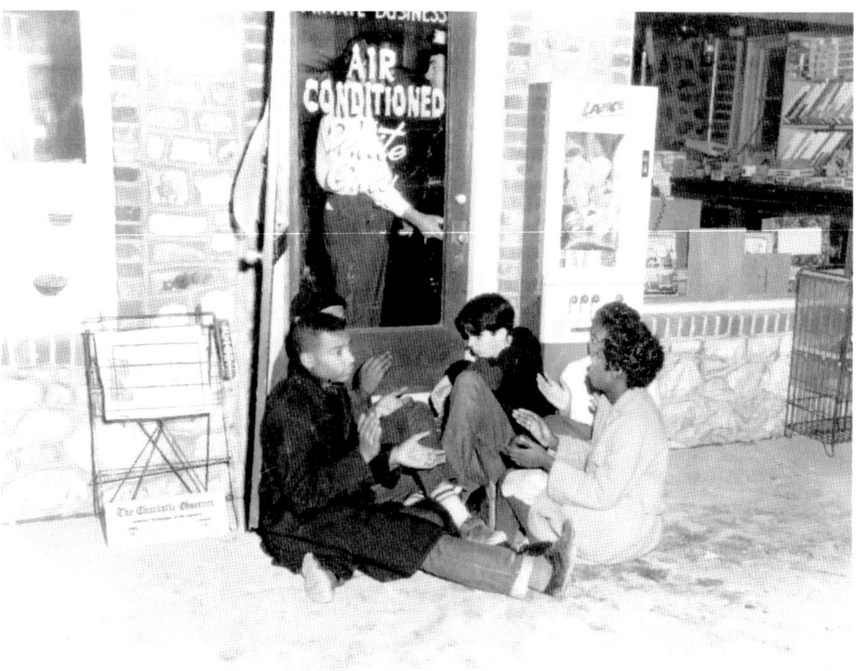

A civil rights demonstration in Chapel Hill on January 4, 1964. This may be in front of Carlton's Rock Pile Grocery at the corner of East Franklin and Estes Drive. Copied from a print loaned by the Chapel Hill Police Department. *Courtesy North Carolina Collection, University of North Carolina Library at Chapel Hill.*

other servile positions imaginable, while finding comfortable housing in the community in which they eked out a living—mostly separate, never equal, to the whites of town—until perhaps late in the century.

Jane Toy Coolidge, born in 1901, wrote:

> *To a child growing up in Chapel Hill in the early nineteen hundreds it was obvious that the world belonged to white people. Colored people were a part of the everyday scene, but always in the background. They were treated considerately, often loved, but never taken very seriously. This attitude was prevalent among most adult whites too, and seems to have been accepted by both races. There was no conflict between them, and no apparent awareness of racial problems. If black people had differing views on this score they kept them quiet, pursuing the jobs open to them and often performing them so well and with such dignity that they were highly respected members of the community. In times of trouble they turned to their white friends for help, and this was given according to the paternalistic tradition of the South. By such personal, individualistic measures white citizens tried to do their duty by their black neighbors.*

Before things got better, things got worse here and all over the nation after the 1954 U.S. Supreme Court ruling *Brown v. Board of Education*, in which it was declared unconstitutional for state-sponsored schools to continue separating the races. But integration took longer in the South. In Chapel Hill during the 1963–64 school year, three young men forced open the racial can of worms through organizing and demonstrating, but to little apparent end other than a significant number of arrests. Still, these events pushed people to think about what side of the issue the town and university belonged on. The Federal Civil Rights Bill was passed on July 2, 1964, and when Paul Sharp arrived as new chancellor from the Midwest in September 1964, he faced a rule instituted in 1963 by Chancellor William Aycock that stated that black students—there were ninety-one that year—were to be segregated from white students in dormitories. John Ehle wrote in his 1965 book, *The Free Men*:

> *Chancellor Sharp, when he encountered this rule, could have nodded and let it alone, but he did not. He announced that the university was discarding the rule, not because of a law or Federal contract, but because it was morally wrong. He said he was taking the action on his own authority without consulting any committee.*

When school integration happened in the Chapel Hill schools in 1966, nobody was more reluctant for it than the black children, who were pushed from the comfort of their neighborhood schools into the hostile environments that forced them to feel their minority. Children were forced to lead the way, soon followed by the youth of the town, bolstered by progressive professors and emboldened blacks who demanded that the laws of the land be honored and that local merchants stop refusing service based on race. Throughout, some people quietly (or loudly) did the right thing, leading the way for progress to rule the day and the quickly growing town, which in 1960 had 12,573 residents and town limits covering an 8.4-square-mile area.

WHITE STUDENTS AT NORTHSIDE ELEMENTARY

In September 1966, Chapel Hill saw its biggest jump in school enrollment to date with 3,533 students and 219 teachers. The newly constructed Chapel Hill High School opened its doors (albeit a few days late) to 950 students. Guy B. Phillips was the only middle school, with 1,095 students, and there were six elementary schools.

The significance of 1966 was that it was the first full year of integration.

Two schools were in their last years of existence as full schools—Lincoln and Northside Elementary. These were the schools for African American children. There were 304 students at Lincoln and 174 at Northside, the smallest school in the system. "It was a sad year," said then Northside principal James H. Peace. The school, which opened in 1951, had seen its heyday during the 1950s with enrollments in the 700s. "Small schools in rural areas had closed in '51, and they came into schools in Chapel Hill." Northside was the only black school at that time, with grades one through eleven. "We had our own little world, a complete culture," Peace said.

It was during this last year that the Ted Cloak family moved into the neighborhood, and the three Cloak children transferred in from Glenwood Elementary. These would be the only three white children to attend Northside. "We bought the house at 121 Kenan Street," Connie Cloak said while on a visit to Chapel Hill in January 1998. "The nearest public school was Northside, and my parents wanted us to attend the neighborhood school." The house was an ideal location for her father, an anthropologist at UNC, who wanted to be able to bike to campus. Going to Northside felt quite natural to the Cloak children. Ted Cloak had done his fieldwork in Trinidad, British West Indies, and the children had attended an all-black village school. When they first moved to Chapel Hill, they had rented a house and the children had attended Glenwood. "There was only one black child in the school," said Connie Cloak, forty-one at the time of the visit. That seemed strange to the Cloak children, who were each two years apart, with Connie in fifth grade, Danny in third grade and Stephanie (called Lynnie at the time) in first grade.

"We fit in very well," Cloak said. "Mrs. Butler was my teacher. She was a loving and warm person and a very gifted teacher." Cloak remembers discussions at the time about the quality of education that the children were getting. "We all three had good teachers that year. They were very nurturing for my sister who was learning disabled. Mrs. Butler was among the best teachers I ever had. She was terrific."

Catherine Butler started teaching in Chapel Hill in 1961, where she taught for thirty-one years and three months. "I remember that year. Chapel Hill–Carrboro had gone about integrating," Butler said. Her husband, Al, is the owner of Butler's Garage in Carrboro, and she knew the Cloak family through his business. "I was a bit surprised when Connie walked in. She was really a bright little girl, and the children accepted her."

The Cloak children walked to and from school. Once they crossed Rosemary, "Church Street was paved but not the other streets. After school we would walk and play along the way and go into each other's homes. Some homes where I visited seemed more impoverished than what I'd seen in a third-world country." Cloak remembers dark, crowded, small rooms that were "shack-like…I felt embarrassed because we had so much." One

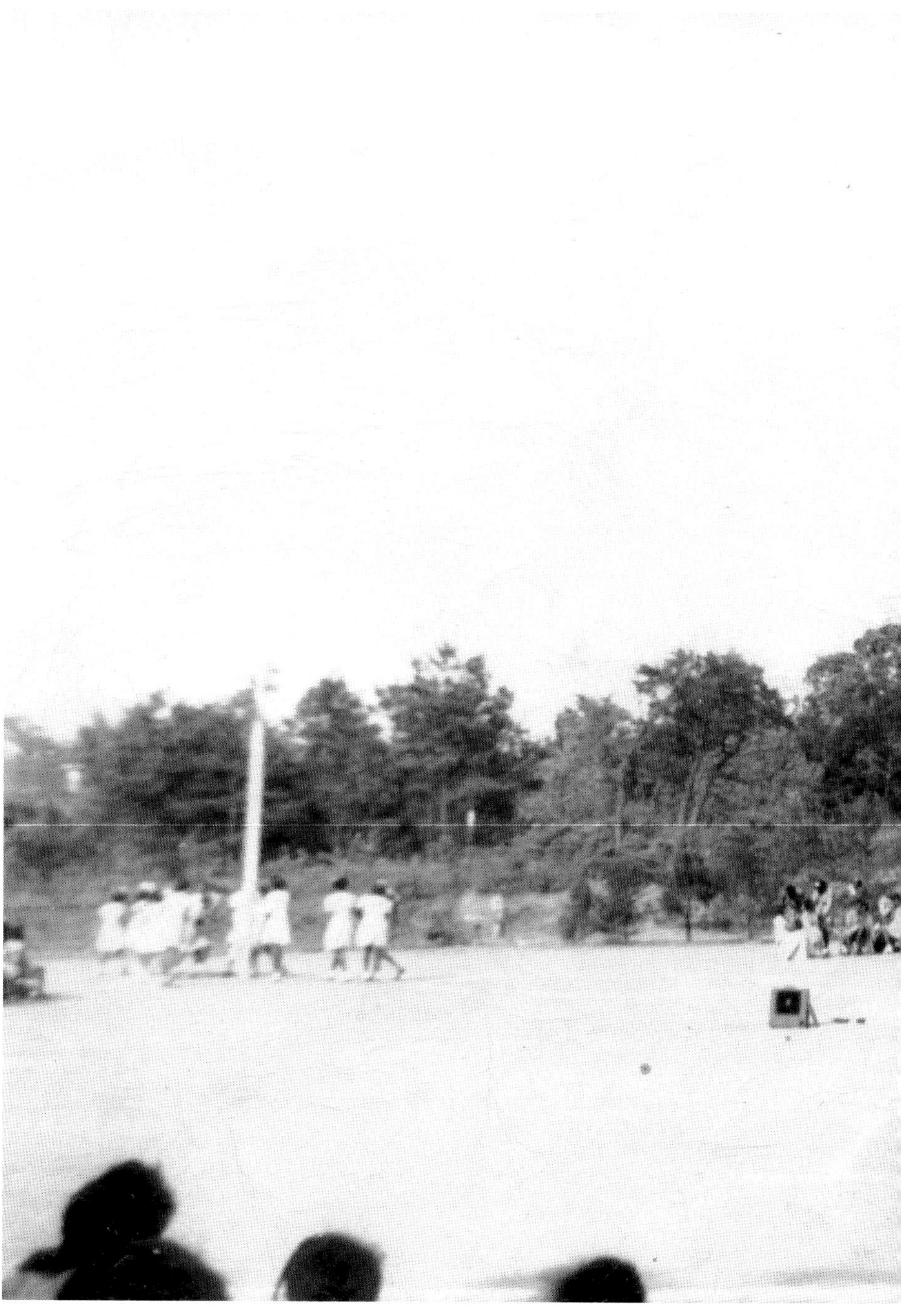

This photo was taken years before the Cloak children attended Northside Elementary, but it shows a long-loved tradition of dancing around the Maypole on the playground at the school. *Courtesy Hargraves family.*

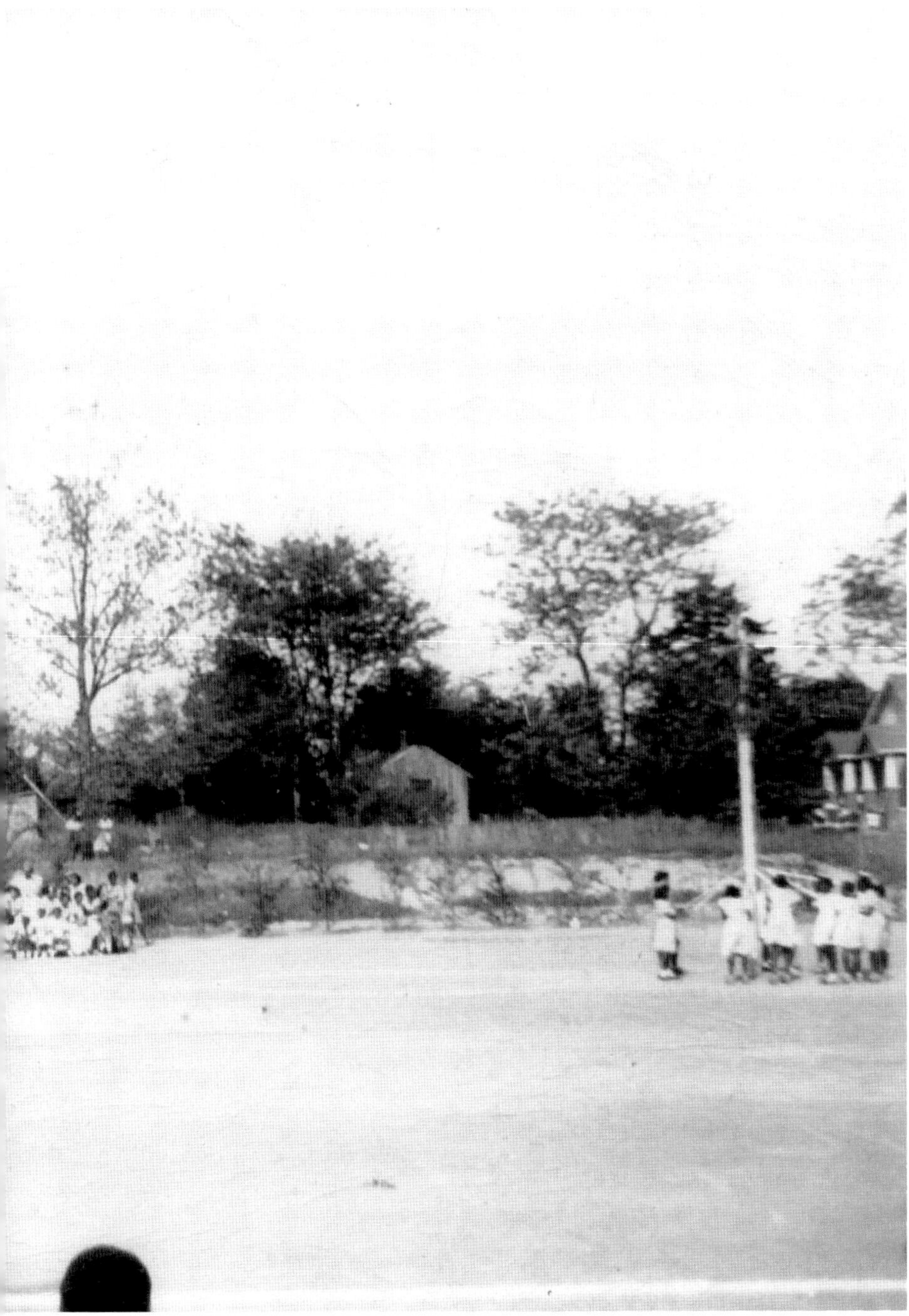

exception was the home of a little girl who had been adopted by an older, well-established couple, who were better able to provide for their daughter.

Inexplicably, Connie was chosen to play Mary when Christmas pageant time came around. She remembers how distraught her mother was when she arrived for the performance and saw that a white baby doll was cast as Jesus. She dashed out of the school and ran over to the house of the adopted little girl, hoping she would find what she needed—a black baby doll—and she arrived with it in time for the pageant. "My parents were the only white adults there," Cloak said.

None of the Cloak children had any problems being accepted at Northside, but "we weren't prepared for how strange it would seem to people in Chapel Hill. My parents were told they were using their children to further their own political ideals." The most difficult time came the next year when, for one year, Lincoln was a combined fifth- and sixth-grade school. "I was the only one who knew both black and white kids." The white kids made it difficult for her. A teacher at Frank Porter Graham would later make third grade unbearable for Lynnie, who said that she was mistreated for her parents' liberal views. "I was so glad to be switched to Mrs. Carmichael's class at Estes Hills," she said recently.

In seventh grade, Connie went to Phillips, and on the first day of school made a friend for life. She and Karen Davis began a friendship that still brings Cloak back to Chapel Hill, although her family left in 1971. Cloak and her husband, Chris Carrieri, own an environmental consulting business in Santa Rosa, California. They return to town regularly to visit Davis and her husband, David Tate. "Chapel Hill is so different now," Cloak said. "There are the same buildings, but they are upscale places. The only place I saw that isn't more affluent is the house I grew up in." She still doesn't understand the closings of Lincoln and Northside. "The schools that were most centrally located were closed because they didn't want the white kids going to black schools."

Lincoln High School Reunion

The sun of a hot Saturday afternoon in July 1998 could not wilt the greetings emanating from the Hargraves Recreation Center. As soon as the first squeal of reunion rang out, it was obvious that this was a group of people who were happy to be back in a community with those they hadn't seen in a while. A tradition begun in 1973 and that happens every three years continued as more than three hundred graduates of Orange County Training School and Lincoln High School, the two names given the pre-integration all-black high schools, gathered for their eighth reunion. Events included class gatherings at homes and restaurants on Friday evening, seeing the newly opened gymnasium at the Hargraves Center Saturday and dressing to the nines and dancing Saturday night at the Omni Europa Hotel. Sunday brought a special time of remembering those whom they'd lost with a memorial service at First Baptist Church; finally, Monday afternoon featured a cookout at Snipes Farm.

Community has always been most central to the African American population of Chapel Hill. More than half of those attending the reunion had relocated to places such as New York, Washington and Detroit, but they all enjoyed coming back to their hometown.

Cletus Clark comes back for each of the reunions. For the past thirty years he has spent his workdays in the White House. "I was in the right place at the right time," he said of how he came to be the decorating coordinator, working with the past six first ladies. From Nixon to Ford to Carter to Reagan to Bush to Clinton, "All the first ladies have been very, very nice and treated us exceptionally well—as have the presidents." Clark has four trades: presser, painter, paperhanger and furniture refinisher. "I do faux refinishing as well, which is good because the more faux the better, they really like that."

He said that he had stayed out of trouble growing up in Chapel Hill, as most people did back then. That was important because, as he said, "Getting a job in the White House requires a perfectly clean record." Clark's wife, Carolyn, also graduated from Lincoln High in 1955. "We started dating in eighth grade," she said. "We'll celebrate our fortieth anniversary next year." She'd retired from working for the federal government and had become an active volunteer. She said her husband had three more years until retirement. "Retirement is not for me at this point," Clark said. "I'm going to go into the next administration."

They were very happy living in the upscale community of Mitchellville, Maryland, where they intended to stay after retirement, but they enjoyed

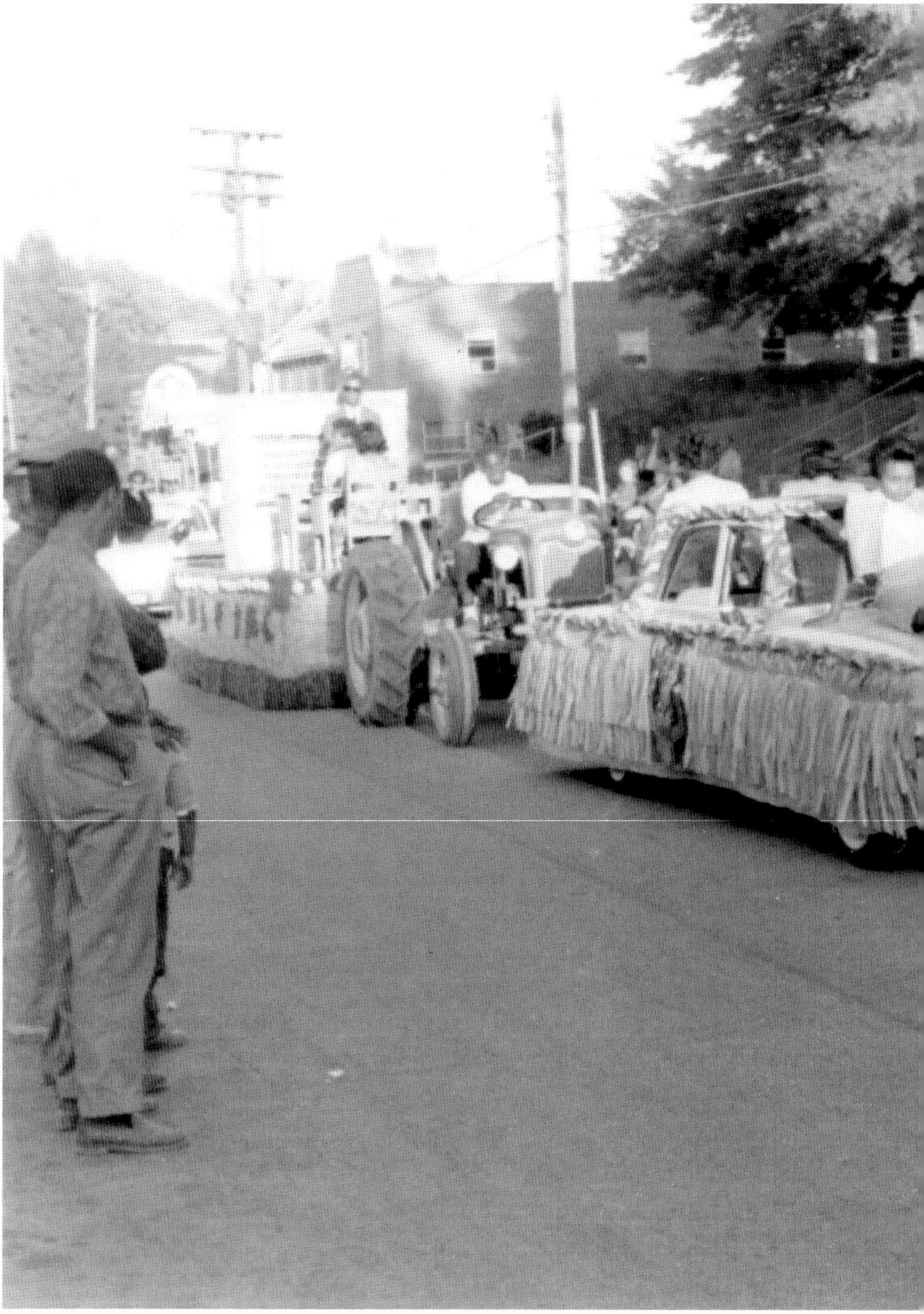

An Orange County Training School parade in the 1960s on West Franklin Street in front of the home in which Frances Hargraves grew up—the house on the right, up the hill from the man on a bicycle—which is today a McDonald's fast-

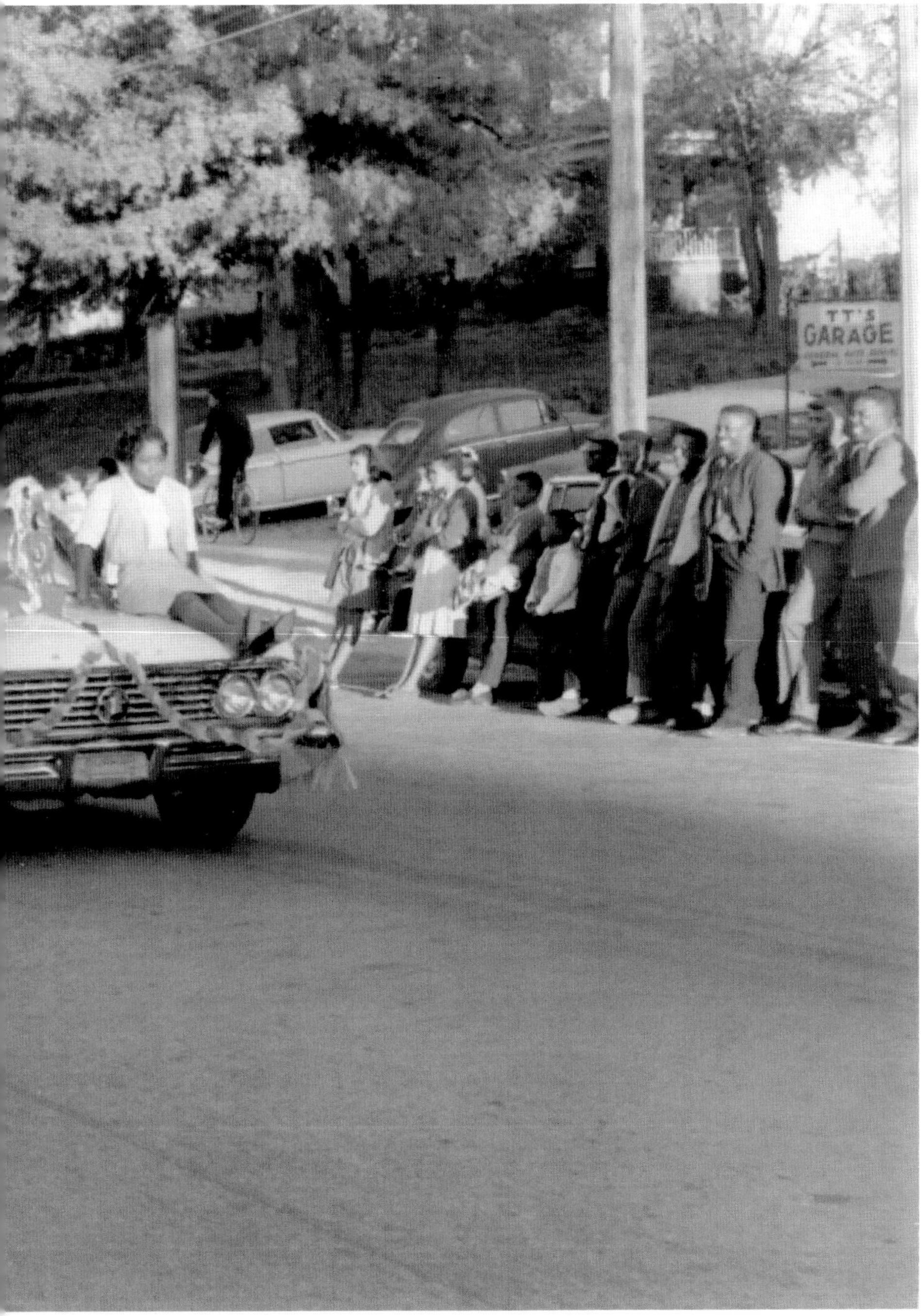

food restaurant. Notice the brick building, which today is where Hazmat and the Internationalist Bookshop are located. *Courtesy Hargraves family.*

coming home. "It's nice to be here in Chapel Hill. It's a very unique place, like one big family where everyone's concerned about each others' lives. There's a closeness in a small place like Chapel Hill, and it's an honor to be able to take part in it now."

Donald Bynum, class of 1958, had lived in Chapel Hill all his life. "There were fifty-five in my graduating class," he said. His three daughters all graduated from Chapel Hill High School, and he feels that something was lost because of integration. "Culturally, it was better (when we were all together). We were sort of bonded. We'd have fights sometimes, but it would be over stupid things." There was no racial tension. "My daughters went to integrated schools and didn't get the experience like we had of having the community."

Alfred Perry (aka "Bro" Perry), class of '51, moved to Raleigh in 1960, where he had been a Wake County principal for twenty-five years. He still owned Chapel Hill property, including the barbershop that his father ran at 111 North Graham Street (then a beauty parlor). "The integration of schools was good, though there were hidden agendas on both sides," Perry said. He received his education in all-black schools until he went to UNC and North Carolina State for postgraduate work. "Blacks felt the system owed them more." He spoke of having to use hand-me-downs, used books and materials. "We had to rework things to make them usable." But the teachers made special efforts. "The teachers were really dedicated to seeing that you got your work done and took more time with us. Late bloomers today get lost in the shuffle."

Some of the graduates had returned to live in Chapel Hill in retirement. Elaine Norwood, class of 1954, went to college in Lynchburg, Virginia, and then moved to New York, where she worked in retail for twenty-one years. After her father died in 1979, Norwood came back to take care of her mother. "I don't regret it," she said. She spoke of the strong sense of community that she has known here and that she never felt in New York. "In New York, I was a southern girl without an accent," she said. "They didn't understand that. I didn't understand their lack of hospitality." Norwood said people who grow up in Chapel Hill don't develop strong southern accents because of the university's influence with so many people moving here from elsewhere. But she grew up learning southern politeness and graciousness that she found lacking in New York. "I was

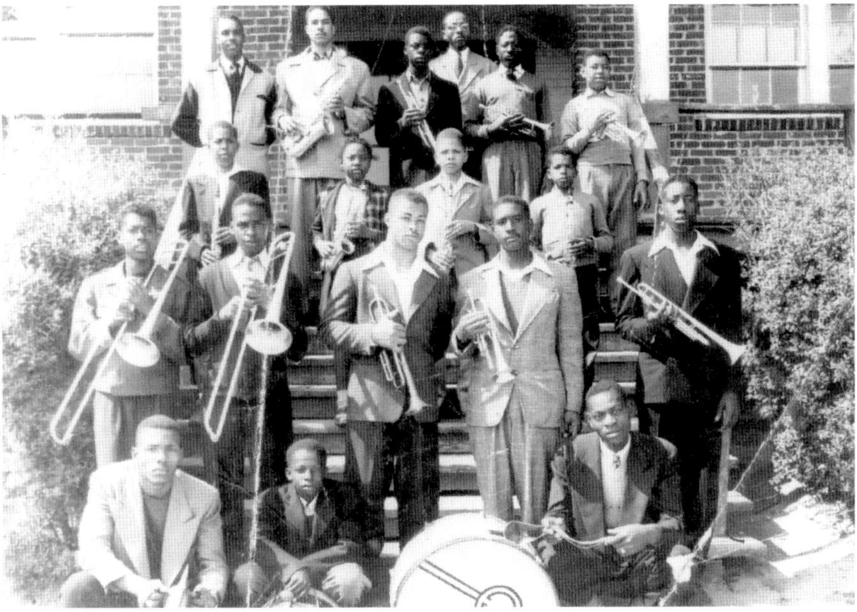

This photo shows the Lincoln High School band members, circa 1950. *Kneeling, left to right*: Samuel Boyd, Matthew Mason and Matthew Farrington. *First row*: Joseph Hargraves, Riley Barnett, Norman Barbee, unidentified and Isiah Foushee. *Second row*: William Hargraves Jr., Bessyne Ward, John Clark and Edwin Caldwell. *Third row*: Otis Pettiford, Melvin Scales (teacher), William McCauley, McArthur Alston and Thomas Purefoy. *In back*: Harry Pickard (teacher/bandleader). *Courtesy Esther McCauley.*

determined I'd never be a New Yorker," Norwood said. "I changed a lot of people. People where I worked [at Tiffany's and Elizabeth Arden] learned to say good morning to me."

Ed Caldwell was one of the organizers of the reunion. "Every year, there's a lot of enthusiasm," Caldwell said. Standing next to a giant charcoal grill at Snipes Farm, men were turning hamburger patties and huge hot dogs. "At the last reunion, the women told us that the men would be cooking this year," he said. "'We're sitting down,' they told us." And so they were. They were sitting in the covered pavilion and indoors, with their families (some with four generations attending) and old friends. Even for those who hadn't left Chapel Hill, they have traveled far.

FRANCES NEAL HARGRAVES

Frances Hargraves spent her entire life, except for her high school and college days, in Chapel Hill, yet she helped lead her people about as far as anyone here ever has. Frances frequently provided representation of the black community during her service as a teacher and, after retirement, on boards and committees. Early in life, she figured out the score and furtively fought to even it up through sacrifice, dedication and love for all—except for those acting through intolerance or ignorance. Frances shared her story from the time we became friends in 1997 until her death on April 16, 2002.

She was born April 21, 1914, in the same two-story house where her mother, Alice Whitted Merritt Neal, was born on March 23, 1893. The house at 407 West Franklin Street was the home of Alice's grandmother, Hester Taylor, but since 1975 that site has been where many a college student has gone for what they might consider comfort food—where McDonald's now stands. It's hard to imagine the farm with pigs and chickens where Frances and her mother and previous generations grew up.

Alice's father, London Whitted, was a teacher of science at Shaw University, and her mother, Emma, was a well-organized housewife, raising six children until her and London's untimely deaths; then Grandma Hester, a strict disciplinarian, raised Alice and her siblings. Alice would be married and widowed twice, living, giving birth and dying in Grandma Hester's house in 1959 at age sixty-six.

Alice began her lifelong career at age fifteen when she went to work in the home of Dr. Will MacNider, a doctor and teacher at the university medical school. In his house, located at the corner of Franklin and Henderson Streets (the site of the post office), Alice developed her love for cooking, which would help her provide for her two daughters. Pearl was born after Alice married Dennis Merritt at age sixteen. Shortly after Pearl's birth, Merritt died. Alice married Henry Neal, and four years after Pearl, Frances arrived.

Alice's skills as a cook and housekeeper were so well known throughout the village that the university offered her a position at the home of President Harry Woodburn Chase, where she worked for five years,

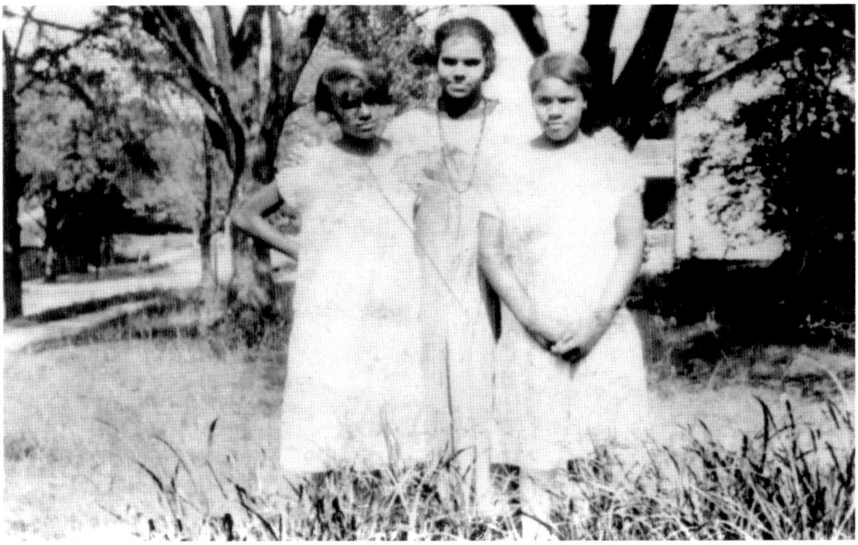

Alice Neal and her daughters—Pearl, age sixteen (left), and Frances, age twelve (right)—in front of their house at 407 West Franklin Street. *Courtesy Hargraves family.*

exposing her daughters to the white world when she could. "Dr. Chase was a northerner. In the summertime, I would go to work with my mother and play with his daughter, Beth. We were as close as sisters. We would eat lunch together every day," Frances said. "Once, when they were having a dinner party, [Beth] asked if I could stay for dinner. It was explained to her that I couldn't eat in the dining room because I wasn't white. So, she took me upstairs and put powder all over me then took me to her mother saying that I could eat in the dining room now because I was white."

That was in the twenties among educated whites. Frances remembered that when Alice Neal was hired by the Chapel Hill School Board as manager and cook in a white public school cafeteria, going to work with her mother became a very different experience than going to the president's house had been. "I found out there are differences in where a person is born," she said, indicating the contrast between northern and southern attitudes—and educated versus incognizant. "I had been so well received by the children of professional parents." But she was taunted by the schoolchildren. "I had never heard the name *nigger* before."

Yet her mother had compassion for the needy children, and not a day went by that she didn't give out free bowls of soup. "It's so hard to change attitudes," Frances said. "They would say that blacks couldn't learn anything, but they never taught them anything. Human qualities weren't acceptable." She explained how whites who were publicly supportive of blacks were called names. Politicians had to avoid race issues if they wanted to win the political race, so the black vote was not pursued.

Before desegregation, West Franklin Street and the area north of it called Potter's Field were where the African American community thrived. The name Northside replaced Potter's Field after the school there was named Northside. West Franklin and West Rosemary Streets were the center of the black business district. "We had to rely upon black businesses to provide the services we needed," Hargraves said. "As a child my mother pointed out a lot of places that were for white people only. There were schools, movies, swimming pools and parks. You entered through the back door, the side door or no door. You learned to live with and accept these conditions."

While still running the school cafeteria in 1930, Alice was approached by the university to work for the new president, Frank Porter Graham. She accepted, and it was, according to Frances, the best decision she ever made. "Dr. Frank lavishly praised Mama for her cooking, mostly Southern cooking," she said. "After Dr. Frank married Marian [Drane, in 1932], she wanted Mama to try some fancier dishes and Mama told her, 'Dr. Frank won't like that.' But Marian brought her a recipe for stuffed tomatoes and said, 'Oh, let's try this.'" Alice told Marian that Dr. Frank liked his tomatoes sliced, but she fixed it anyway. "She stood in the crack of the kitchen door watching him push it around, playing with it," Hargraves said, chuckling. "He didn't like it, and Mama jumped up and down."

Pearl's son, Edwin Caldwell Jr., grew up knowing Graham. "Dr. Frank would open his house to students on Sundays, and any kid could come and meet with him," Ed Caldwell said. "Since my grandma worked for him he would ask me to come in and meet him. He would ask about my grades and aspirations, and he always stressed education. When he left UNC, he would come back and visit Grandma and sit on her porch at 407 West Franklin Street. I was much older and in college, and he still stressed education," Caldwell recalled.

During this time, Frances graduated from the Mary Potter High School in Roxboro and then married William "Willie" Hargraves, whom

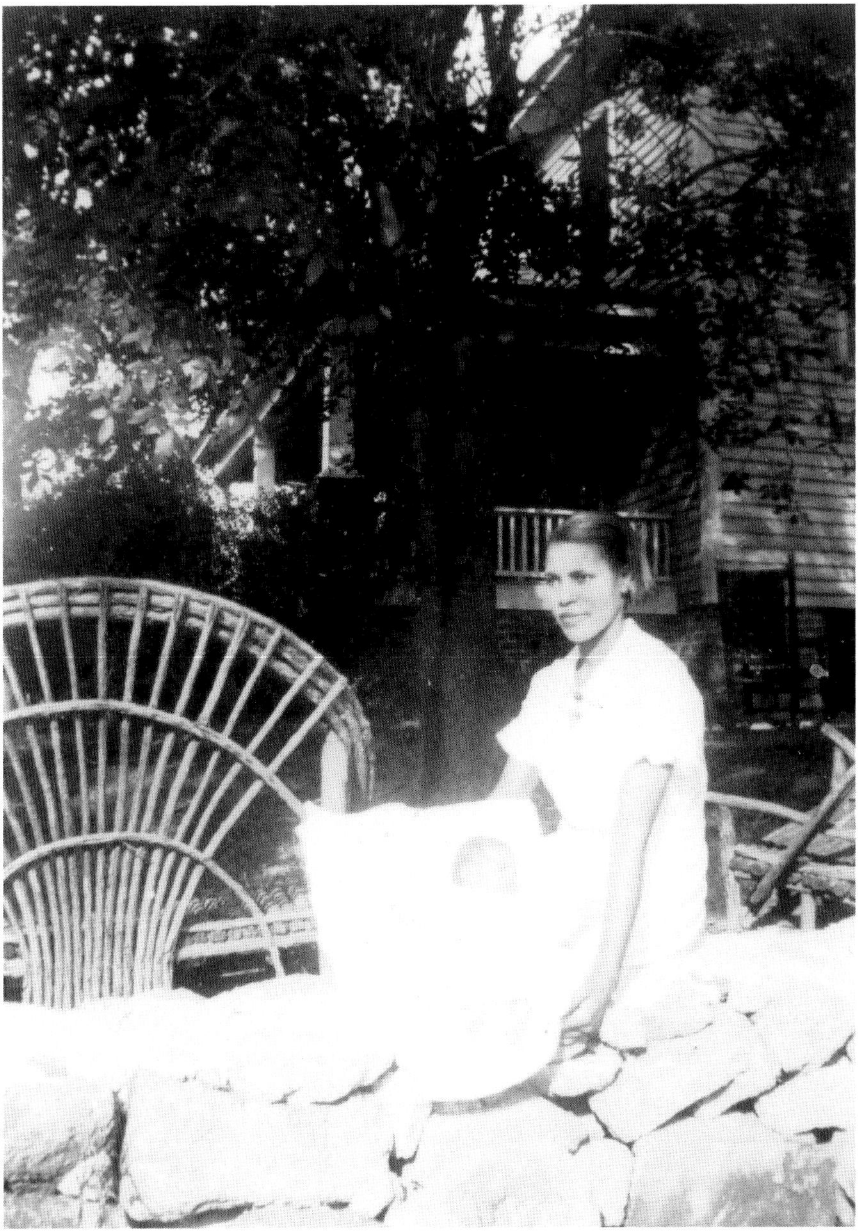

Frances Hargraves sitting on a rock wall next to her West Franklin Street home on July 26, 1936, with Alice Geraldine, at age five weeks. *Courtesy Hargraves family.*

she'd known all her life, a graduate of the Orange County Training School. William used his skill with the saxophone in local clubs by night and worked at the Chapel Hill Post Office by day. "They weren't hiring blacks as clerks yet—only as janitors," she said. They started their family, with William Manning Hargraves Jr. born on May 16, 1934, followed by Alice Geraldine born July 26, 1936. After the children had started school, Frances continued her education at Winston-Salem State College (now University) and remembered one bus ride home in 1944. "I was sitting next to a white woman from Chapel Hill when a white man got on, and the bus driver told me to give the man my seat," she said. "The white lady told me to stay." But the bus driver was insistent. There were no other empty seats. "The white lady stood up and said to him, 'You can have the whole seat.' We stood up from Burlington to Chapel Hill," Hargraves said. In 1946, Frances started teaching in Chapel Hill.

Soon after, a most difficult period for those close to Frank Porter Graham began with his campaign for U.S. senator in 1950. He resigned as university president when he was appointed to finish the unexpired term of the late Senator J. Melville Broughton. When he ran for a full term, he was one in a field of four, and the campaign of one of the candidates, Willis Smith, was being run by Jesse Helms, previously news director at WRAL radio. It was an ugly campaign that played on the anxieties of white voters toward race and class. One campaign poster that stood out in Hargraves's mind was a picture of Marian Graham sitting among a group of black men. "The caption read, 'If you want this to happen to your daughters, vote for Frank Porter Graham.' Helms hated Dr. Frank's guts," Hargraves said. "And Helms denied all of it. Mama would say, 'That man's going to keep me out of heaven' [for what she was thinking]. I told her, 'Mama, you don't hate him as a person, you hate what he's saying and doing.' Mama told me she was trying to work toward that." Helms later become a five-term Republican senator, serving from 1973 to 2003.

"Uncle Frank was ahead of his time," Hargraves said. "He was such a wonderful man; he was just born during the wrong time." But she recognized that the strides that were made back then were only possible because of people like Graham.

In the late 1950s, when a new elementary school needed a name, the school board decided to approach Graham for permission to name it after him. Dr. Kemp Jones, who was chairman of the board at that time, said, "Frank Porter Graham was a great man, and very few things had been named after him. We felt it was very appropriate." The Reverend Dr. J.R. Manley, the first African American school board member and pastor of the First Baptist Church, the largest black church in town, went to Jones's office and they made the call to Graham at his office in the United Nations in New York, where he spent much of his career after losing the Senate race. "He returned the call and said he would be proud to have it named after him. He said it would be an honor," Jones said. Manley said that Graham allowed his name to be used on the school because "he felt we were moving in the direction upon which his principles were based. This was going to be such a fine school, anybody, black or white, would be allowed to go there to get a good education."

Mary Scroggs was chair of the school board when Frank Porter Graham Elementary School opened. She remembered one thing: "We couldn't name it for him if it wasn't desegregated."

William "Billy" Manning Hargraves Jr. was educated in the Chapel Hill school system, graduating from Lincoln High School in 1951 (he's in the photo on page 95) and from Hampton Institute in Hampton, Virginia, with a bachelor's degree in physical education. He served in the U.S. Army and worked in a correctional school for boys in Illinois. He broke the color line as the first black person hired to work with the public at the U.S. Postal Service in Chapel Hill. "They hired him as a clerk," Hargraves said. Even though he had a college degree, it was a victory in those days. He met his wife Glenda after she got a job at Duke and moved into the Caldwell Avenue house next door to Frances and Willie. They married in 1967 and had two children, Malcolm and Veronita.

In the community, Billy was known especially for volunteering daily at the Roberson Street Recreation Center. When he died at age thirty-nine as the result of a car accident on Rosemary Street on February 5, 1973, the Chapel Hill Board of Aldermen voted unanimously that day to rename the center in his memory. Two years later, his father, Willie, died after a long illness, exacerbated by the loss of Billy.

A year later, Frances Hargraves retired from teaching and began her next career as a volunteer and ambassador for her community. She had taught school for thirty years; in 1966 she had become the first black teacher at Glenwood Elementary, where she taught white children for the first time. She remembered well the first parents' night and how nervous she had been. "There were so many parents and there weren't enough chairs," she said. She became the special education teacher, and kids who the other teachers couldn't do anything with came to her. Little was known about learning disabilities then, but one of her greatest assets was the ability to bring out the best in people—a gift for her students.

The gifts she gave the town during retirement, though, knew no bounds. She served as a board member for Orange County Women's Center, Chapel Hill Preservation Society, Chapel Hill Museum, Delta Sigma Theta, Delta Kappa Gamma, Golden Age Happy Circle, Women of Distinction of Orange County Extension Homemakers Club, Mental Health Association of Orange County, the American Lung Association, Meals on Wheels and Northside Residents Advisory Committee and was a volunteer with RSVP (Retired Senior Volunteer Program) for twenty-six years. At St. Paul's AME Church, where she grew up, she was on the board of trustees and taught Sunday school for fifty-three years. She was named Chapel Hill–Carrboro Council of Women's Organizations' Woman of the Year in 1985 and the Chapel Hill–Carrboro Teacher of the Year in 1971. She was an Olympic torch carrier through Chapel Hill during the 1996 Olympics; was named an Unsung Hero by the Abundant Life, Seeds of Sheba Cultural Center; and won forty-four medals in Senior Olympics games.

The medals were indicators of her mettle. She had started walking in her sixties at her doctor's encouragement and soon walked two or more miles per day. Alice Battle, a cousin of Hargraves who was raised by Frances's mother, recalled going on a 1991 trip to Ohio with Hargraves, twenty years her senior. "Aunt Frances said, 'Come on, let's walk over there,' and she pumped up her arms close to her side like she'd do and off she went," Battle said. "Those arms propelled her. I had to run to keep up with her."

In 1998, a wish that had been stated decades earlier came to fruition through the work of Frances and her nephew, Edwin Caldwell, who, as survivors of the family, served their communities to their dying days.

Ed, who had been the second black to serve on the Chapel Hill–Carrboro School Board (he was appointed after losing two elections), received word in 1971 that Graham wished to see him. "He was staying with his sister after Miss Marian died, and he had shingles and was wearing a baseball cap," Caldwell remembered. "We talked, and he'd been following me on the school board and he told me he had one request—he wanted the library at Frank Porter Graham Elementary to be named after Alice Neal." This put Caldwell in a jam as the board had just created a policy that no more schools would be named after people. "I hemmed and hawed and said I'd see what I could do," Caldwell said.

A while later, Graham's sister, Kate, called Hargraves. "She told me, 'Frank's failing quickly, and he still has on his mind to name the library after Alice,'" Hargraves recalled in July 1998. She and Caldwell went over and besides talking about the naming, he punctuated it by talking about buying books for the library. Even after that, Caldwell couldn't bring himself to say anything to the school board—the request, which he would be making for his grandmother, would go against this new policy—even if he had thought policy might be broken, he couldn't imagine that it would be for anyone black. He also knew that not everyone agreed with Graham's liberal views. Caldwell kept it to himself.

In the mid-1990s, the media specialist (librarian) at Frank Porter Graham Elementary School, Barbara Dewey, called Caldwell and asked if he would speak to a group of Girl Scouts about the history of the school. He agreed to and, during his talk, mentioned Graham's request. The Girl Scout leader became very excited about the idea of having the library dedicated and took the idea to the School Governance Committee, but as it was the end of the school year, nothing more happened. Dewey also heard what Caldwell said and spoke to school governance member Mary Phillips about it. Phillips said that in order to move forward with it, some kind of confirmation of Caldwell's claim had to be made. As things go in small towns, a short time later Dewey heard Hargraves speaking at the Chapel Hill library and realized for the first time that Hargraves was Neal's daughter. After speaking to her, she got the confirmation required. "Naming the library after Alice Neal had been a dream of Frances Hargraves's family for years and years and years," Dewey said. She, Hargraves, Caldwell and Phillips all wrote letters to the School Governance Committee, and the request was granted.

"Dr. Frank was one of those people who knew the system wasn't functioning right," Hargraves said. "He had a human heart and feelings about people. It wasn't easy for those who stood up for what they believed. Many can't understand the turmoil of people who went through the era of segregation."

Seven months later, Hargraves collapsed after a luncheon event for two hundred people that she had worked hard to produce, at which Senator Howard Lee had given the keynote address. "I was just happy I didn't fall out until after the luncheon was over," she said. "The Lord held it off." After finding a large mass in her left lung, her doctor gave her a few weeks to get ready for surgery. Hargraves also prepared to die, but following surgery on March 24, 1999, the news was pretty good. Though the tumor was malignant, it had not spread and had been removed. No further treatment would be required once she recovered from surgery.

Chapel Hill attorney Robert Epting provided a lift in Hargraves's recovery—a flight over the village in his airplane from the Horace Williams Airport, little more than a mile from her home. "Frances Hargraves reminds me of my own mother, who was a schoolteacher," Epting said. "I feel connected to her." She was in awe as they flew over her beloved Chapel Hill, over McDonald's—the site where her family had lived for so long—over Hargraves Center, Northside Senior Center, which was once the first black school in town, over her home, the UNC campus and Frank Porter Graham Elementary School. She said she had flown over Chapel Hill before in the 1950s, when the school system had arranged flights for teachers. By comparison, she said, it looked like a big city, maybe a little too big. Student housing was overwhelming her own Northside, which had belonged to the black community since the end of the Civil War. Since the late 1960s, outsiders had been offering ever-increasing amounts to buy the homes. Houses were often razed, with duplexes or small apartment buildings built on the lots. "Northside is being swallowed up," she said. "The future for the black community looks bleak right now if something isn't done."

She kept doing, reading weekly to children in the day-care center at the Northside Senior Center and stirring every pot she could to create improvement, but three years later—during which her daughter, Alice, a nurse, had died of pneumonia, and a few weeks shy of her eighty-eighth birthday—her cancer had returned. While still in the hospital, the subject most on her mind was children—beyond the preschool children—the children caught in the "achievement gap," as some minority children in the Chapel Hill–Carrboro school system have been described. "They talk about closing it," Hargraves said of the gap. "You'll come close, but you won't close it. You have to go back to the roots, and nobody's saying that." She knew there would always be a group made up of very successful black children, where the parents had learned the value of education and exposure to cultural venues. "It's fine to do academics, but you need to throw in cultural exposure, language skills, social skills. When I taught special education students, I taught my children social skills. I took them to lunch at the swanky Carolina Inn and made them feel good about themselves," Hargraves said of the twenty years she taught special education.

"She made a difference for every one of those children," said Virginia Kitzmiller, who was the principal at Carrboro Elementary when Hargraves taught there. "She made a real difference for them."

Florence Peacock served on the boards of the Chapel Hill Museum and the Preservation Society of Chapel Hill with Hargraves. "She always attended meetings, never missed one, and her input was always positive," Peacock said. "She would say incredibly astute things about how to improve things. I respect her greatly and love her sense of humor."

Joe Herzenberg had known Hargraves since the early 1970s. "She was always so friendly and wanting to help with whatever the project was," he said, noting that Hargraves's attitude made a difference. "I just always enjoyed working with Frances."

A month before Hargraves's illness returned, a group of those she had worked with had put their heads together to do something special for her, which became "A Tribute to Frances Hargraves" at the Horace Williams House. "Frances has been involved in so many committees and activities for the betterment of all the community," said State Senator Eleanor Kinnaird. "She has created so much with her presence, energy and creativity. We just wanted to make a tribute to her—to our beloved Miss Frances from all her friends and the community. Her work has been all-encompassing," Kinnaird said. "She's a true treasure to our community."

A few weeks before the celebration, I visited Frances at home, where she then spent most of her time in bed. She decided to get up, and as she sat on the side of her bed, gathering her strength, she told me how she had been thinking about her mother and how much she had continued to accomplish up to the time of her death. "Then I realized," she said. "Mama was only sixty-six years old when she wore out!"

Three hundred people showed up to pay tribute to Hargraves on the sunny Sunday afternoon a few days before her eighty-eighth birthday on April 21, 2002. Through great effort and supported by her family, Frances made it as well, arriving in a pink suit, slipping at the last moment out of cozy blue house slippers into matching pink shoes as the wheelchair she sat in was rolled out onto Horace Williams's porch, where she greeted her adoring public. "Frances absolutely was waiting for that day," said her niece, Velma Perry. She knew the planning that had gone into it and didn't want to let anybody down but let her friends know that she was holding on for the day of the tribute.

Facing the crowd, her daughter-in-law, Glenda Hargraves, fanned her throughout the abbreviated ceremony as her nephew, Edwin, introduced the speakers, among them Lieutenant Governor Beverly Perdue (who would become North Carolina's first female governor in 2009), Senators Howard Lee and Ellie Kinnaird and Orange County commissioner Moses Carey. After the accolades were over, the microphone was handed to Frances, who said, "I prayed for this day to be what God wanted it to be. All that I did was because you opened doors for me. I couldn't do what I did without your support…I hope my living will make a difference."

Not thirty-six hours later, she got up from bed during the night, collapsed and died. Upon learning of her death, former Chapel Hill mayor Rosemary Waldorf remembered that Hargraves would walk by town hall and sometimes stop for a visit. "She was not there to complain," Waldorf said. "She was a great example to everybody of how to be uplifting. She's one of those people for those of us who knew her, who'll always be with us. Hers was an absolutely unforgettable spirit."

Melvin and Zora Rashkis

Melvin and Zora Rashkis both knew their callings early on. "I was two years old when I announced I was going to be a teacher," Zora said. "I never wanted to be anything but a teacher."

Mel, who at the age of sixteen had moved with his family from New York to Canada, started his real estate career when he returned from three years of service in the Canadian army during World War II. Mel built a summer camp on land that he and his father bought. "It was 160 acres of land with two miles of lake frontage," Mel said. "I had to buy all the materials for it on the black market." In 1949, as he was traveling through Cleveland on a promotion trip for his lodge, a mutual friend introduced him to Zora. "I was intrigued," Mel said. Zora, who was widowed, had two children, and Mel invited them all to make the six-hour drive up to Muskoka, Ontario, during the summer.

Zora accepted the invitation.

"That put the seal on it," Mel said. The following year they married. A picture hanging in their home testified to the fact that it was a good decision—it showed the family of four in the lodge kitchen during a candid moment in time, captured with smiles and happiness beaming from their faces.

In 1953, Mel sold the lodge and camp, and the family moved off to Cleveland, where Mel began selling real estate. After the children were grown, Mel branched out into the prefabricated housing business, which led to their move to Chapel Hill in 1962. "I was traveling more than we enjoyed, then I received the offer to come here," Mel said. "Our move to Chapel Hill was the best thing that could happen to us. It was such a pleasure; everybody was so friendly and appreciative and there have been so many opportunities to do things."

In quick succession, they fell in love with Chapel Hill, with a parcel of land near Estes Elementary School and with the contemporary home they built made of undetectable prefabricated sections. Wasting no time, they established themselves in the community—through Mel's real estate business and Zora's school teaching—and as active volunteers throughout over forty years as residents.

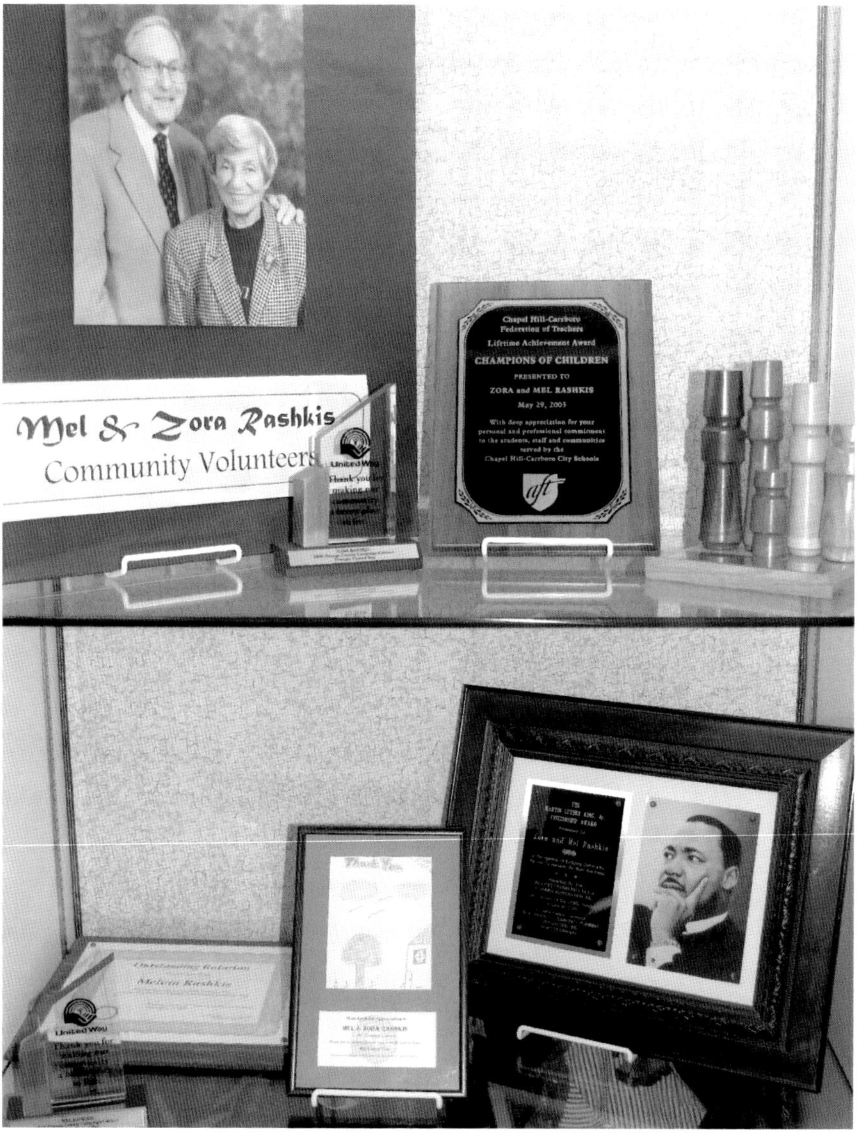

The Mel and Zora Rashkis display, with some of their awards, located at the elementary school named after them. *Photo by Valarie Schwartz.*

In 1965, when Howard and Lillian Lee moved to Chapel Hill from Savannah, Georgia, only one real estate agency would show them a house in any section of town—or show them any courtesy or respect. "I grew up as a sharecropper's son on a farm eighteen miles southeast of Atlanta and only six miles away from Stone Mountain, a stronghold of the Ku Klux Klan," Howard Lee said. "I used to dream of belonging in society beyond certain positions." Mel Rashkis provided the first sign that Lee had found his nirvana in Chapel Hill when the young couple turned to the Mel Rashkis and Associates Real Estate Agency.

"Mel Rashkis instructed his staff to always do what he did, and that was to treat all people with respect and dignity," Lillian Lee recalled. Zora used the same approach with the children she taught at Phillips Middle School. "Zora would invite students from her class, regardless of race, gender or religion, to her home so they could get to know each other as people and each other's cultures." The students' parents had to come as well. "When you get to know each other outside of the classroom, it's easier to be accepting and friendships are formed," said Lillian, also an educator.

Zora introduced her students to other cultures through trips that she took with the students each summer. Students who committed to going on the trip had to earn the money for it themselves. "They learned what it meant to work for money," Zora said. The Rashkises' basement had become a museum of sorts with Zora's collections of dolls and other relics from student trips around the world.

Before she retired, Zora began a cablevision program called *Meet the Teacher*, highlighting the work of teachers and school administrators. She volunteered as host of the show every week for twenty-two years until 2002.

As for the Lees, they never forgot the open hearts and minds that they experienced from Mel and Zora. Perhaps it was that introduction to Chapel Hill that galvanized Howard toward his successful career. In 1969, spurred by the burning of a cross on the lawn of their Colony Woods home and supported by an organization of black leaders including Edwin Caldwell, Lee won the election against Roland Giduz by four hundred votes to become the first black man elected mayor in a predominantly white southern town, prodding his dream and that of all

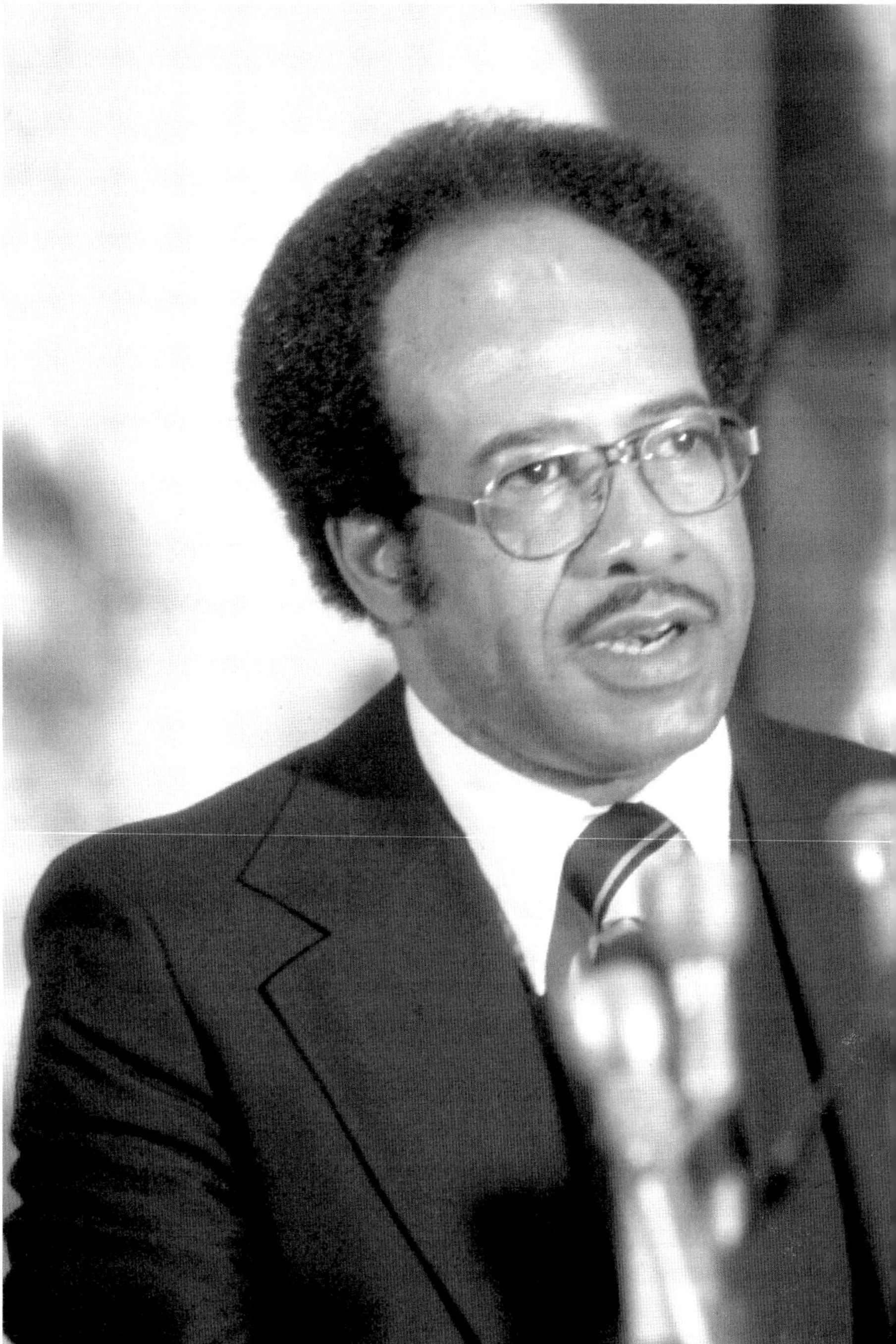

Howard Lee as he ran for mayor in 1969. *Courtesy Billy Barnes.*

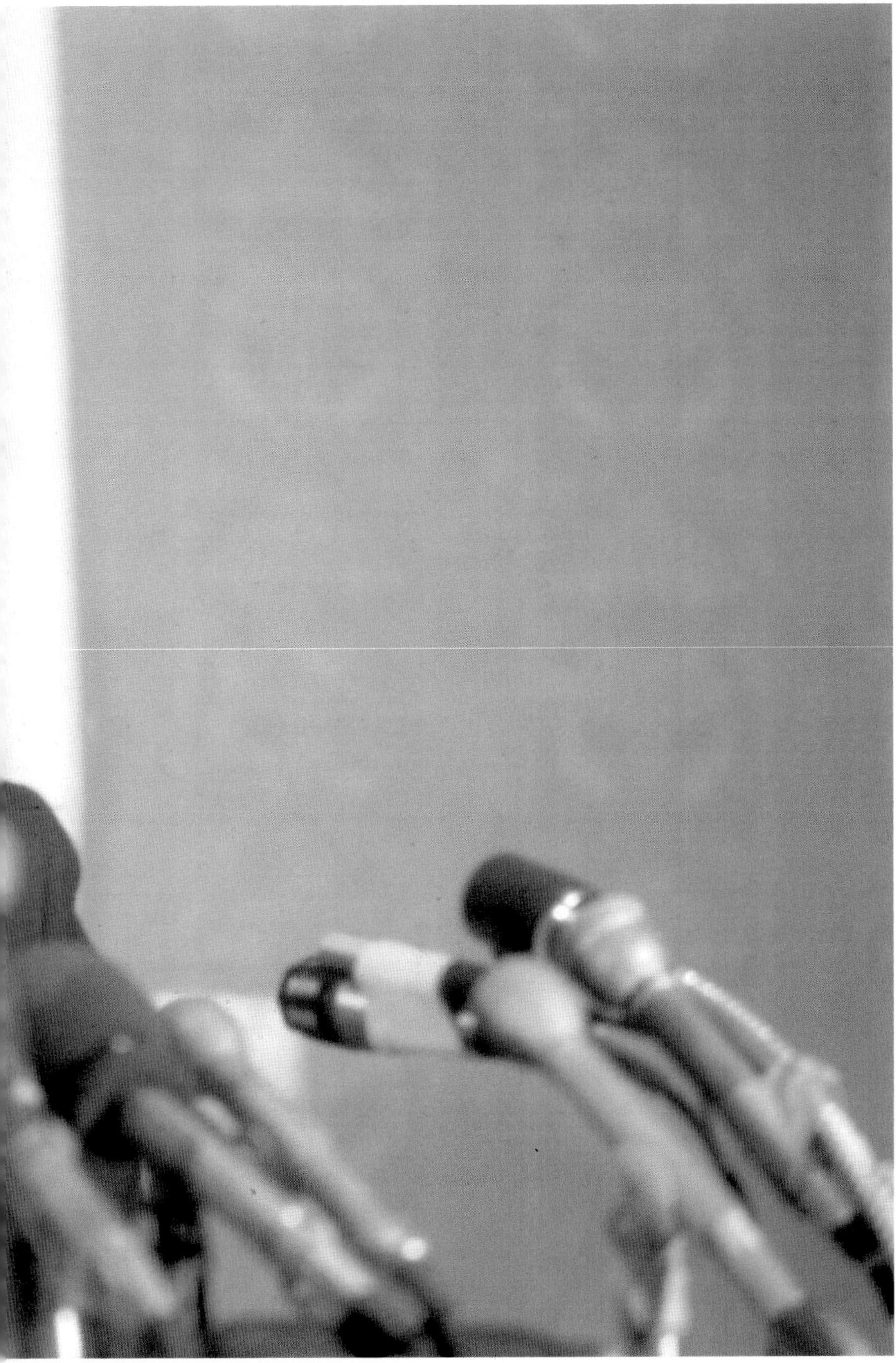

African Americans a nudge closer as he served three and a half terms during turbulent years. Among other things, a successful city bus system was established during Lee's tenure. In 1977, Lee became secretary of the North Carolina Department of Natural Resources and Community Development, appointed by Governor Jim Hunt, a position he held until 1981. In 1990, he was elected to the North Carolina Senate, where he concentrated on public education issues from 1990 to 1994 and from 1996 to 2002. In 2009, Governor Beverly Perdue appointed him as new executive director of the North Carolina Education Cabinet.

Lillian also maintained a career that earned her great respect. She had already been named "Teacher of the Year" in Savannah, where she had been the second-born in a family of eleven children. "Growing up was not easy," she said in her calm, quiet, Lillian way. "The main ingredients were love and encouragement—and encouragement came in many different forms," she said as she peered over her glasses, making sure the point was made that some lessons got learned the hard way. When children of her family did something wrong, they were sent to the peach tree to pick a switch. "If you picked one too small, you were sent back for another, and the two were twisted together to make a really nice thick one," she said, smiling her beautiful smile. Something in the lessons stuck, since ten of the eleven children went to college. "Daddy told us all the time to work hard and get an education."

The Lees raised three children of their own, but in thirty-two years of teaching in the Chapel Hill–Carrboro School System, Lillian helped raise many others, especially ones who struggled as they reached Chapel Hill High School, where she held titles like competency/remediation teacher, alternative program teacher, detention and in-school suspension teacher—and dean of students, from 1979 until retirement in 2000.

"Kids today are struggling with so many different issues they did not create," Lee said. "They don't have the kind of respect for teachers they once had, and the way they dress is unbelievable. Some seem not to know what they're going to do or where they're going—much less how to get there." But she recognizes the root of the trouble. "Parents have changed. They are so concerned about being best friends they don't say no. Kids need boundaries and structure throughout childhood—you can't wait until they are twelve or thirteen—it's almost too late. Parents making tough love decisions would make a difference." Her students remember her and she remembers them, recognizing their voices years after graduation when they call her.

Lillian and Howard Lee also remembered the kindness of the Rashkises when it was time to give the Martin Luther King Jr. Citizenship Award presented by the MLK University/Community Planning Corporation in January 2000.

"Mel and Zora Rashkis have given equal access and equal treatment to all people," Howard Lee said at the banquet held at the Morehead Planetarium. "As one of his former employees said, Mel was ahead of his time and that made him special." He said that Zora advised one African American student that she could be anything she wanted if she studied hard and worked to her potential. The student took that advice and was accepted at the University of North Carolina–Chapel Hill. "As she was nearing the end of her degree, tuition was a problem and Zora paid it," Lee said. The young woman received her degree.

On the day in October 2002 when Mel and Zora celebrated her eighty-ninth birthday and their fifty-second wedding anniversary, they received news that theirs were among the names being considered for the new elementary school at Meadowmont. "It's an honor to be recognized along with the other very wonderful people being considered," Mel said. "Win or lose, we've enjoyed the experience of being suggested." They won, and the school was built less than a mile from the Cedars retirement community where they had moved. Visiting the school became a new pastime for the couple, and it was where they donated Zora's collection of dolls from her past travels with students.

Mel said that over the years Zora was named outstanding teacher in the state of Ohio and outstanding English teacher in North Carolina. "The Public School Foundation named a chair after her," he said proudly. Mel did his fair share of work for the schools as well, most recently starting the Community Alliance for Student Success with the objective of bringing parents and students closer together—which led, among other things, to providing computers in the homes of students who could not afford them and computer training for their parents. Mel and Zora could be counted on as audience members at every theatrical production at Chapel Hill High School, and at Mel's suggestion, PALs (Performing Arts Lovers), the parent support group of its Performing Arts Program, was started as a means to raise money for its programs.

From the time they arrived in Chapel Hill and became involved in the project of building a reform temple (Judea Reform Congregation), to jointly receiving the United Way Citizenship Award in 2000 and the Martin Luther King Award the same year, these two served their community and became favorites of anyone who worked with or knew them.

At least one Rashkis story became something of an urban legend —except that it's true. Zora's daughter, Jill, was an infant when Zora's first husband died. When Jill was three, Peter arrived, but not by normal methods. "I found Peter on our doorstep," Zora said. She opened her front door and on the mat was a blue-eyed, red-haired nine-month-old baby boy in a basket. "I figured that if that was what God intended for me, then we were going to adopt him." Then, when Jill was eight and Peter was five, Mel became the man of the house and the family was complete—at least until Mel and Zora became the grandparents of seven and great-grandparents of six.

"We've just enjoyed doing everything we can with and for the community," Mel said. Melvin Rashkis died on November 8, 2008.

Joe Nassif

In 1964, Joe Nassif moved to Chapel Hill intent on using the degree in architecture that he had earned at North Carolina State University that same year. Before military service, he had previously received a degree in civil engineering from the University of Notre Dame, so when he hung his shingle on the house at 220 West Rosemary Street, he offered clients and the town a sizeable amount of knowledge. Five years later, he began public service to his new hometown (he was born in Laurinburg and raised in Wilson) when he was elected to the board of aldermen (now town council). Town hall was then located at the corner of Rosemary and Columbia Streets in the same building that today houses the Inter-Faith Council Shelter for the Homeless; it was little more than a block from his office.

"Everything was in there," Nassif said of town hall. Filled to the brim, the building held the police station, the fire station and the courtroom, and the jail was located in the basement, where prisoners would sometimes disrupt meetings with their carrying on. Nassif's first meeting as an alderman was Howard Lee's first meeting as mayor, when both were to be sworn in on a hot August night in 1969.

"I walked into the courtroom and it was jammed with people and television cameras, and it was so *hot*!" Nassif said. It didn't take long for him to catch onto the fact that not only local but also national and international news companies were there to cover the induction of Howard Lee—the first black mayor of a predominantly white southern town. "It was a big thing in that hot little courtroom," Nassif remembered. Two years later, Lee was running for his second term when, once again, television media had the place covered as Nassif arrived for a meeting, and he asked Lee if he had called a news conference. "Howard said, 'No, they've got my opponent locked up in jail, and *he's* holding a press conference!'" The board members had a hard time settling down to business that evening—they were so tickled that the only way Lee's opponent could get any attention was by getting himself arrested.

Nassif animates his slowly paced words with his native accent, adding details where needed, always leading to his point. After the Chapel Hill Greenways Commission gave him a Vision Award in June 2001, he sat down and talked to me about his years of service to the town, as alderman from 1969 to 1973 and mayor from 1979 to 1985.

"Chapel Hill was, in my opinion, still not on a par with the university," he said. "The university had all the utilities, the town was a stepchild; the budget and town were very small. The town had not faced the realities that growing causes." He said the town had needed upgrading, and he became the one-man committee for sidewalks. Except for the business district of East Franklin Street and Glen Lennox (a garden apartment complex that had been built a few years after World War II), the town had no sidewalks. Dirt walkways were the pedestrian areas for West Franklin and Rosemary Streets; Airport Road (now Martin Luther King Jr. Boulevard), which was then two lanes, had dirt shoulders. Nassif started with sidewalks for the areas around schools and continued getting things paved through his two mayoral terms. "Widening the 54 bypass was one of the last things

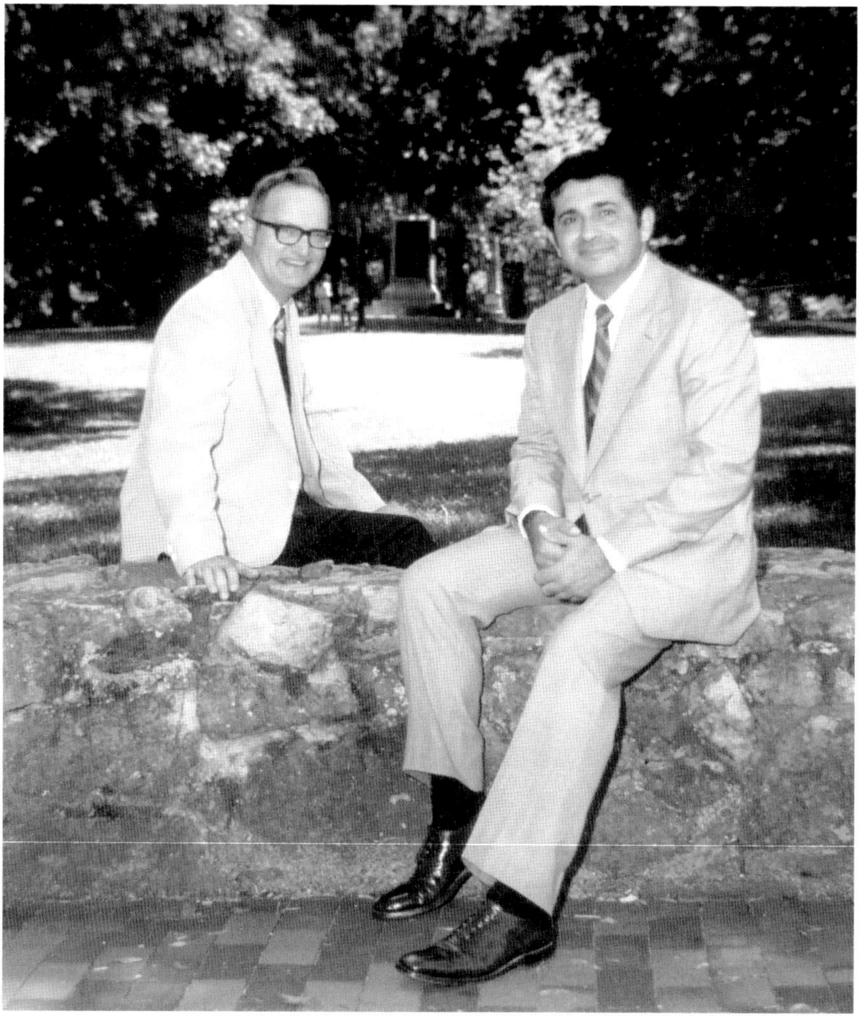

Newly elected Chapel Hill mayor Joe Nassif sits on the "town" side of the campus rock wall with newly appointed chancellor Chris Fordham sitting on the "gown" side, 1980. *Photo by Orville Campbell, courtesy Joe Nassif.*

I did as mayor," he said. The four-lane divided highway that shepherds traffic away from residential areas through Chapel Hill and Carrboro as NC 54 had been a two-lane horror of bumper-to-bumper traffic. "Oh, you wouldn't believe it," he said.

The most controversial issue Nassif faced during his years in public office was the acquisition of land to form Cane Creek Reservoir. Since the days when running water and power had become available, the university had owned the utilities. But as the town grew, UNC decided to get out of the utility business. "We decided we wanted to have it," Nassif said, speaking for the town. "The university didn't want us to have it. We wanted to be an 'electric city' and sell to the citizens." Nassif said that the town tried like the dickens to make it happen but it was not to be. The university awarded Duke Power the electricity and water, but Duke Power didn't see fit to mix the two, refusing the water. So, in 1975, the Orange Water and Sewer Authority (OWASA) was incorporated—the first integrated water and sewer authority in the state—and in February 1977 it assumed ownership. Everett Billingsley, who had served as chief of operations for the water and electric utilities at the university, was hired by the OWASA board as its first executive director, a position that he held until 1996.

While the OWASA was being formed, the state experienced a tremendous two-year drought. Expansion of the university and the town coupled with low rainfall strained the 600-million-gallon-capacity University Lake—the only potable water source—prompting discussions of postponing opening the university for classes for the fall 1976 semester. Besides strict conservation measures, the only thing that kept water running was the ability to purchase water from Durham after two pipelines had been laid along U.S. 15-501 in 1969.

Many believed that a new water source had to be sought. "We were in a crisis situation and water supply was a key public issue," Billingsley said. A key player was Dan Okun, a professor of environmental engineering, who began his teaching career at UNC in 1952. By his third year at Carolina, Dr. Okun saw evidence that by the 1960s there would be a water shortage because of the area's growth. He began assigning advanced degree students in one of the courses he taught the task of identifying the best future source for drinking water, a practice that by 1968 proved that the Cane Creek area, eleven miles west of Carrboro off NC 54 West, would be the best option. Okun's testimony before the Environmental Management Commission, as well as urgings to the Corps of Engineers, helped establish the direction away from the other options and toward taking advantage of the land in Bingham Township, where a community of farmers had prospered since the eighteenth century, establishing the Cane Creek Baptist Church in 1789.

"Cane Creek Reservoir would be essentially a protected water supply source in perpetuity, whereas Jordan Lake water quality had a far greater opportunity for degradation as a result of growth and development," said Pat Davis, who has served on the OWASA board between two occasions of working for OWASA, most recently as utility manager generalist.

Primarily dairy farmers, some of whom had been passing their land down in the family since the 1780s, were not about to allow their livelihoods or lifestyles to be disrupted without a fight—not even for use by the university, from which some had graduated and which most held in high regard. One family had even named their farm Anilorac (Carolina spelled backward) for the university down the road. Besides farmers, there were also university professors and other professionals, as well as a colony of so-called hippies, enjoying the quietude of life away from town. When members of the OWASA board went out to Bingham Township in 1977 and met with the landowners, Everette Billingsley let them know that the decision had been made to build the lake out there and told them when the surveyors would arrive, when the timbering would begin and where and when the dam would be built. With the launching of this first barrage, the two hundred or so "country" people attending the meeting left and immediately began their counterattack, which started with organizing the Cane Creek Conservation Authority (CCCA) and hiring a lawyer, who instructed them to allow no surveyors on their property. All factions of the Cane Creek community came together in defense of their territory.

Shirley Marshall, an Orange County commissioner and OWASA board member, was at the meeting and later expressed sympathy for the people of Cane Creek. She said she was "appalled" at the way they had been treated, though she still believed that the project was the best and only decision the town could have made.

Jimmy Wallace was mayor of Chapel Hill at the time, and he supported getting the water from Cane Creek. Then, in 1979, Nassif became mayor. He had been off the board of aldermen for six years and needed updating.

"Joe sent his administrative assistant out to interview me—it was Rosemary Waldorf, who had been with the *Chapel Hill News*. It was my first meeting with Rosemary," Billingsley said of Waldorf (who would serve as mayor of Chapel Hill from 1995 to 2001). "Her style was very low-key, but she gave me an intensive, extensive interview about the situation and possible alternatives of supply and the pros and cons of Cane Creek Reservoir. She prepared a briefing paper and evidently did an excellent job." Waldorf's paper showed Nassif the need—and pointed out where to go for the best drinking water source: the Cane Creek area in Bingham Township. There were other options: expansion of University Lake or taking chemical-laden water from the Haw River in Chatham County or from Jordan Lake (a reservoir, which would not be filled until 1983, though the dam was finished in 1974).

"Joe Nassif played a key role in helping the community understand the importance of pursuing Cane Creek Reservoir rather than selecting Jordan Lake as the source for water," Davis said.

"Joe did extremely well," said Anne Barnes, former state legislator and manager (along with her husband, Billy) of Nassif's mayoral campaigns. "He has a good sense of humor and a quick wit—both of which are an advantage in public service. He was good at finding common ground where it was possible and was able to make people feel their opinions were appreciated."

The way Nassif saw it, "I kept going to public hearings and getting booed." The battle waged on for nearly a decade, with the country neighbors inviting the townspeople out for "Farm-City Days," where they would sell barbecue, ham biscuits, pies and cakes and raffle off a quilt made by the local women. The Cane Creek Cloggers—a dance group still in existence that preformed around town, raising money and awareness of the issue—was organized and included Okun's daughter, Tema—on the other side of the issue from her father.

"The neighbors used every angle they could to reject the project," Davis said. But one agency after another granted OWASA permission as every completed study showed Cane Creek as the area with the greatest potential and ultimately least amount of impact if acquired then, instead of twenty or so years down the road.

"It was because of their wonderful stewardship of that land as farmers that it was as clean as it was and as attractive as it was and some of the best dairy farming land in the state of North Carolina," said Bob Epting, a founding OWASA board member who has served as its general counsel since 1984.

Eddie Mann may have been the person in the greatest bind during the entire process. He shared some of his experience at OWASA's twenty-fifth anniversary celebration on February 28, 2002, saying:

> *Since I was personally residing in that area; and since my wife was a member of a farming family which was one of the landowners in the project area and also active with this opposition organization* [CCCA], *I had a very intimate knowledge of the local side of this issue. And as an OWASA Board Member I was in a unique position to be a messenger and negotiator, almost exclusively in a behind-the-scene role. Very often during Board meetings, I would have to absent myself and refrain from any involvement in the decision-making regarding land acquisition. Our attorney, Bob Epting, was adamant about this need to avoid any real conflict of interest or any appearance of a conflict of interest…*
>
> *It is sometimes difficult for a non-farmer to understand how these farmers actually feel about their land and their unabridged freedom to use it as they see fit, and why they would be so passionate about defending it from being acquired. For periods of time going back, in some cases, two hundred years, these families have lived in this area, worked the soil, depended on it for their food and their occupation, raised families, and in general become intimately intertwined with it and heavily dependent upon it. Furthermore, farming is a physically demanding occupation and way of life, and the thought of new regulations, which would restrict the farmer's ability to use his own judgment in his business are feared and hated. OWASA's efforts here to take some of their land from them and to regulate what remained provoked a lot of emotion. It was OWASA's plan early on to avoid actually using any condemnation procedures if at all possible in order to minimize the potentially harmful effect on the people and the community and OWASA's ongoing relationship with them. One could say that in the end all of the landowners were able to negotiate the sale of their land to OWASA in an honorable and non-threatening manner.*

Still, Nassif recognized the pain for the neighbors and the lack of choice for the town. "We had to have a source," he said. "It was the best source around."

In December 1988, Cane Creek Reservoir was completed at a total cost of $17 million with a storage volume of approximately three billion gallons of water covering a thirty-two-square-mile drainage area and a surface area of 540 acres. The estimated safe yield was ten million gallons per day, which has been adequate enough to serve the ever-expanding population even during severe droughts (with conservation measures in place).

It was through service with the Jaycees that Nassif, the father of four, got into public service. "I had not the vaguest thought of running for office," he said. "I was approached by David Etheridge, and he asked me to run and talked me into running for alderman." Howard Lee unknowingly persuaded him as well.

"Roland Giduz [Lee's opponent] and I had shown up at the Jaycees meeting to make a speech, and I convinced a lot of people to vote for me for mayor," Lee said. It was one of those occasions where spirits were high and when he spoke, everything came out right. "Joe came up to me after the meeting and said, 'I think I'm going to run for the board of aldermen.' I had not known Joe well until we started running together. He was a fantastic alderman," Lee said.

"I was involved for sixteen to eighteen years," Nassif said. "When I was through being mayor, I cut out all that stuff." He returned to being an architect and now considers himself semiretired. His kind face formed a gentle smile as he thought back on his days in office. "I liked all those people I served with," he said. "They are special people, good people even if we didn't agree. After we finished arguing we'd have a beer. Nothing was personal."

EPILOGUE

Throughout the process of writing this book, Tar Heel basketball games were something to look forward to each week. My memory can't provide another season when I've been able to catch every single game (from an ancestral chair in front of the television). Even after they hit their nadir, losing the first two ACC games following a brilliant pre-conference season, the team inspired me, proving that anyone might falter or slump while pushing through to completion of a challenge.

As I finished the book, the Tar Heels, led by the incomparable Roy Williams, found their way to the pinnacle so long sought, and they returned home victorious, the NCAA trophy in hand. The can-do spirit abounds in Chapel Hill, and I leave readers with one last Chapel Hill-ism.

Those who live here often refer to our town as the "Southern part of heaven," a phrase for which I hadn't known the origin before my recent delvings. It was coined following the death of the much-loved downtown merchant Adam Alexander Kluttz, known to folks as "Doc" Kluttz. He had completed the two-year medical training at UNC, but without the means to move elsewhere to further his studies, he made a life here and never lost the moniker. He and Mrs. Kluttz, who were childless, owned the large house across the street from the president's home (it today houses the Delta Delta Delta sorority), where they kept a garden that helped feed the boarders they took into their home.

As the story goes, in 1926, as Doc lay dying in his home, he asked his friend, Parson Moss, who was sitting at his bedside, what he thought heaven would be like. Moss answered that he thought it might be a lot like Chapel Hill in the spring. Doc smiled and said, "That's good," and then died.

We carry the stories and numerous gifts left behind as we carry on our work in this dogwood-blossomed heaven we call Chapel Hill, where history is made every day.

Selected Bibliography

Here listed are some of the publications that helped me in writing this book. Though this bibliography is not a complete record of sources consulted, it includes those from which quotes were obtained or that further elucidated information from interviewees. Much of the content came from stories that I wrote for the *Chapel Hill News*, the *Carrboro Citizen* and *Chapel Hill* magazine.

Blythe, W., F. Denny and W. McLendon. *Bettering the Health of the People: W. Reece Berryhill, the UNC School of Medicine, and the North Carolina Good Health Movement.* Chapel Hill: The University of North Carolina Press, 2007.

Coolidge, Jane Toy. *Growing Up With Chapel Hill.* Chapel Hill, NC: Tri-Printers, 1988. First published 1977 by Universal Printing & Publishing Company.

Ehle, John. *The Free Men.* New York: Harper & Row, 1965.

Henderson, Archibald. *The Campus of the First State University.* Chapel Hill: The University of North Carolina Press, 1975. First published 1949.

House, Robert B. *The Light That Shines.* Chapel Hill: The University of North Carolina Press, 1964.

Love, Cornelia Spencer. *When Chapel Hill Was A Village...* Chapel Hill, NC: Creative Printers, 1976.

Swalin, Benjamin. *Hard-Circus Road: The Odyssey of the North Carolina Symphony.* Raleigh: The North Carolina Symphony Society, Inc., 1987.

Swalin, Maxine. *Coming of Age in North Carolina's Fifth Century.* Chapel Hill, NC: North Caroliniana Society, 2003.

———. *An Ear To Myself.* Chapel Hill, NC: self-published, 1996.

Vickers, James. *Chapel Hill: An Illustrated History.* Chapel Hill, NC: Barclay Publishers, 1985.